Nonfiction Author Studies
in the
Elementary Classroom

Nonfiction Author Studies in the Elementary Classroom

Edited by Carol Brennan Jenkins
and Deborah J. D. White

HEINEMANN
Portsmouth, NH

Heinemann

A division of Reed Elsevier Inc.

361 Hanover Street

Portsmouth, NH 03801–3912

www.heinemann.com

Offices and agents throughout the world

Library of Congress Cataloging-in-Publication Data

Nonfiction author studies in the elementary classroom / edited by Carol Brennan Jenkins and Deborah J. D. White.

    p. cm.

    Includes bibliographical references.

    ISBN-13: 978-0-325-00855-4 (alk. paper)

    ISBN-10: 0-325-00855-8

    1. Children's literature—Study and teaching (Elementary). 2. Prose literature—Study and teaching (Elementary). 3. Authors—Study and teaching (Elementary). 4. Children—Books and reading. I. Jenkins, Carol Brennan. II. White, Deborah Jean Downs, 1954–

LB1575.N66 2007

372.64—dc22
                                            2006034858

Editor: Kate Montgomery

Production editor: Sonja S. Chapman

Cover design: Jenny Jensen Greenleaf

Compositor: Kim Arney

Manufacturing: Louise Richardson

Printed in the United States of America on acid-free paper

11 10 09 08 07 EB 1 2 3 4 5

Contents

Contents

1

Nonfiction Author Studies in the Elementary Classroom

Carol Brennan Jenkins

*Books wind into the heart. . . . We read them when young, we
remember them when old. We read there of what has happened to
others; we feel that it has happened to ourselves. We owe everything
to their authors. . . . Even here, on Salisbury Plain, with a few old
authors, I can manage to get through the summer or winter months,
without even knowing what it is to feel ennui. They sit with me at
breakfast; they walk with me before dinner—and at night, by the
blazing hearth, discourse the silent hours away.*

—William Hazlitt

Curious as to the authors with whom forty-one fifth graders would choose to sit and discourse, I asked them to write a letter to their favorite author. All but one immediately
identified a favorite author and independently drafted a letter explaining their intrigue
(Jenkins 2006). Their favorites ranged from J. K. Rowling, Louis Sacher, and Dav Pilkey
to Mark Twain and J. R. R. Tolkein. In perusing their choices, I was struck by the fact
that all chose fictional authors, despite recent findings that suggest the popularity of
nonfiction among upper-elementary and middle school students (Ivey and Broaddus
2001; Worthy, Moorman, and Turner 1999). While it may be the allure of topic rather
than the allure of author that draws readers to nonfiction, I suspect that this finding has
more to do with the natural tendency to associate the word *author* with fiction. Case in
point are the results of surveys completed by a group of third graders who also were
asked about their favorite author. All but one chose a fiction author. When subsequently
asked about a favorite nonfiction author, thirteen out of nineteen recorded a particular
author, with Joanna Cole winning by a wide margin (Jenkins 1999).

   In all likelihood, the third graders' fascination with both fiction and nonfiction
authors parallels that of readers of all ages. This was certainly true of our second president, John Adams, who had affaires de coeur with both Cicero, Roman philosopher

and statesman, and Shakespeare (McCullough 2001). Adams discovered Cicero's *Orations*, "one of his earliest, proudest possessions," (McCullough 2001, 34) at age fourteen, and he returned to Cicero's essays throughout his life for essentially the same reasons he returned to Shakespeare—to be nourished emotionally and intellectually, to be uplifted by the eloquence of Cicero's language, and to be intrigued by Cicero as person and writer.

The pursuit of literature, both fiction and nonfiction, then, often results in the pursuit of a particular author. When readers find intellectual and/or emotional sustenance in a particular book, they often seek out its author with the expectation of renewed pleasure and engagement. In this chapter, I begin with scenarios of three popular approaches to nonfiction author study. I then briefly trace the historical and theoretical assumptions of these three perspectives and their influence on the current design and implementation of nonfiction author studies in the elementary classroom, grades 1–6. I conclude by advocating a model of *nonfiction author study as multiple response* that respects the layers of response—personal, text-based, and biographical response—that readers bring to an author's corpus of works.

Three Popular Perspectives on Nonfiction Author Studies

As you read the following synopses of three author studies on Joanna Cole, creator of The Magic School Bus series as well as numerous other nonfiction books, note the differing perspectives that the teachers adopt. Following each scenario is a brief overview of the historical precedent for the perspective and how it aligns with the current thinking about nonfiction literacy instruction.

Nonfiction Author Study as Biographical Response

Mr. Van Loan, a third-grade teacher, opens his author study by reading excerpts from Cole's (1996) autobiography, *On the Bus with Joanna Cole*. The third graders learn that the young Cole was an avid bug watcher who loved science and enjoyed writing reports in school. They also learn that The Magic School Bus character Ms. Frizzle was inspired by Cole's junior high science teacher, Ms. Bair, who delighted her students with endless science experiments. After reading these excerpts, Mr. Van Loan draws a spider map on chart paper, places Joanna Cole's name in the center, and asks the children to help him fill in the map with information recalled about the author. The next day, Mr. Van Loan reads the first half of *The Magic School Bus Inside a Beehive* (Cole 1996), posts the Cole spider map, and asks the children to make connections between Cole's life and her literature, which he records on the map with a different-colored marker. The third graders are quick to note that the class is studying about insects at the beginning of the story, using magnifying glasses to observe various insects, writing reports about insects, and preparing to take a beehive field trip. For the remainder of the author study, Mr. Van Loan continues to have the children examine Cole's nonfiction literature through the lens of her autobiography and other biographical sources.

Teachers who design nonfiction author studies in concert with Mr. Van Loan subscribe to the perspective of author study as biographical response. Central to this perspective is the primacy of the author; readers are guided to ferret out the links between the author's life and her literature. As Keck writes about nonfiction author studies: "One of the best parts of an author study is getting to know the author as a person and not just a name printed on the book cover" (1992, 124). Keck recommends that teachers display the author's books and spend the first few days of the author study reading biographical information about the author and making connections to her books.

This perspective of literary biography, which dominated the field of literary criticism from the sixteenth to the nineteenth centuries, placed the author at the center of the literary experience and established the dictum that literature could be understood only within the context of the writer's life and times. Thus, for example, to unfold the true meaning of *The Scarlet Letter*, a reader must focus a lens on Hawthorne's dark, ancestral past. Hawthorne (1850/1967) readily admitted that he wrote *The Scarlet Letter* to atone for the sins of a great-grandfather, one of the judges who sentenced women to torture and death during the Salem witch trials (Bender et al. 1998).

There is no question that literary biography not only illuminates the work—whether fiction or nonfiction—but also heightens our intrigue with its creator. The literature takes on new meaning because we have come to know and care about the author. However, as teachers we need to decide whether we want to launch a nonfiction author study by privileging biographical response—"I'll tell you what I know about this author, then you'll hunt for biographical connections"—over other types of response. As will be argued at a later point, we serve children best when we solicit their thoughts, reactions, and feelings about what they have read (Rosenblatt 1978) before we probe biographical or other types of response. As Northrop Frye noted: "There is a study of literature, or criticism proper, and there is the direct experience of literature. These two are inseparable, two halves of one great whole which is the possession of literature" (1963, 144–45). If Mr. Van Loan values the "direct experience of literature," he will first encourage his third graders to tell their bee stories, express their intrigue or fears, and share their knowledge. Subsequent talk about Joanna Cole and her fascination with insects as well as her writing process, at a later point in the author study, will extend their engagement with *The Magic School Bus Inside a Beehive* as well as their understanding about nonfiction text.

Nonfiction Author Study as Text Analysis

Ms. Valanzola begins her author study by giving book talks on three of Cole's books, placing *A Snake's Body* (1981) on the left side of a large table, *A Chick Hatches* (1976) in the middle, and *The Magic School Bus Inside the Human Body* (1989) on the right side of the table. She then asks her third graders to help her sort other books by Cole. She shows *A Bird's Body* (1983) and asks where she should place it on the table and why. She repeats this process with books such as *The Magic School Bus in the Time of the Dinosaurs* (1984), *My New Kitten* (1995), and *A Dog's Body* (1986). The third graders successfully categorize the remaining books, telling Ms. Valanzola, for example, to place *A Dog's Body* behind *A Bird's Body* because "they are about animals' bodies" and *A Chick Hatches* behind *My New Kitten* because "it's a new chick that has just hatched like a new kitten that's born." Ms. Valanzola then compliments the children on their ability to glean the parallels among books and begins preliminary instruction on two of the primary text structures (description and sequence) found in these books. She tells the class that she will read excerpts of *A Chick Hatches* tomorrow to see if they can identify its text structure. Over the next few weeks, Ms. Valanzola uses Cole's works to introduce other text structures as well as nonfiction features such as headings and bulleted summaries.

Teachers who align themselves with Ms. Valanzola's approach to nonfiction author studies adopt the perspective of author study as text analysis. They believe that the best way to study an author is to study the literature itself. Case in point is Duthie, who, rather than begin her author study on Gail Gibbons with biographical information, privileges text-based response by immersing her first graders in Gibbons' books "in order to become familiar with the author's writing style and subject matter" (1996, 13). (Note: The terms *text analysis* and *text-based response* are used interchangeably in this book.) For example, she directs her youngsters to examine the organizational structure of the how-to book *The Pottery Place* (Gibbons 1987) and the whale chart in *Whales* (Gibbons 1991b) as well as the visual displays used to support the content in *From Seed to Plant* (1991a). No mention is made of investigating Gail Gibbons' life to explore the intersection of her life and her literature or gauging her first graders' personal responses to the works. It is the text that is given center stage in this model.

During the 1930s, opposition to the Romantic obsession with literary biography was sounded by the New Critics, who heralded the sanctity of the text and banished both the author and the reader from the literary experience. New Critics, such as T. S. Eliot, argued that literature, like the Grecian urn, should be judged for its intricate form and its inherent richness. Readers were expected to engage in a close reading of the novel or the poem, analyzing its words, images, metaphors, ambiguities, and so forth. Readers' thoughts and feelings were considered irrelevant to the interpretation of the text, as was the author's life.

Attention to the structural dimensions of text and their impact on children's comprehension and composition blossomed during the 1970s with research in the areas of story grammar and expository text structures. With respect to fiction, researchers found that children as young as four years old who were immersed in stories used their schema knowledge to understand stories and to generate stories of their own with increasing levels of competence, complexity, and sophistication over time (Golden 1984; McKeough 1984; Stein and Glenn 1979). With respect to expository text, Meyer (1975) identified five top-level organizational patterns that illuminate "the logical connections among ideas in the text as well as subordination of some ideas to others" (Meyer, Brandt, and Bluth 1980, 74). It is these patterns (e.g., description, sequence, compare and contrast) that Ms. Valanzola is introducing to her third graders. Such analysis of nonfiction text structures and features is essential if we want to advance children's expository reading and writing. However, the pivotal questions remain: Should we prioritize the "study of literature" over the "direct experience of literature" (Frye 1963, 144–45)? Should we narrow the response to a corpus of work to one dimension (text analysis)?

Nonfiction Author Study as Personal Response

> Ms. Chambliss launches her Joanna Cole author study by reading *The Magic School Bus Inside a Beehive* (1996). During Ralph's (one of Ms. Frizzle's students) report on allergic reactions to bee stings, Tom raises his hand and explains what happened the last time he had an allergic reaction. From that point on, the third graders interject personal responses during the read-aloud. Halfway into the book, Ms. Chambliss decides to harness their excitement by asking them to write about their encounters with bees, which the students share the next day. Their interest is such that Ms. Chambliss announces that she will invite a local beekeeper to class to answer questions and to talk about his hobby. The following day, the third graders perform a Readers' Theatre of the remainder of *The Magic School Bus Inside a Beehive*. Ms. Chambliss designed the Readers' Theatre script by using the actual text from *Inside the Beehive* to create parts for narrators, Ms. Frizzle, and students in Ms. Frizzle's class. Having previously performed Readers' Theatre scripts, the third graders locate their parts, practice their lines silently, and then participate in a class reading. Pleased with their efforts, Ms. Chambliss suggests that they perform it for the other third-grade class. Ms. Chambliss approaches the remainder of the books in the Cole author study by placing the accent on the children's aesthetic responses to the works. The children write personal responses, create murals of favorite book parts, act out engaging content, write letters to the characters giving advice, and so forth.

Teachers who espouse Ms. Chambliss' belief that it is the reader's response to an author's literature that is central adhere to the perspective of author study as personal response. In this perspective, it is the reader in continual transaction with the text that defines the literary experience (Rosenblatt 1978). In fact, Rosenblatt insists that without the reader, there is no text: "A text is merely ink on paper until some reader (if only the author) evokes meaning from it" (1991b, 116). During this process of evocation, the reader adopts one of two stances to the text: aesthetic or efferent. Aesthetic response, also called personal response, occurs during the actual act of reading, when a "reader's attention is centered directly on what he is living through during his relationship with that particular text" (Rosenblatt 1978, 25). An efferent stance, on the other hand, "designates the kind of reading in which attention is centered predominantly on what is to be extracted and retained after the reading event" (Rosenblatt 1988, 12–13). Rosenblatt acknowledges that most reading falls at the midpoint of the continuum; readers attend both to private meaning (personal connections to the text) and public meaning (information to be retained, acted upon, etc.). She is quick, though, to rectify the assumption that fiction is read aesthetically and nonfiction, efferently:

> Instead of thinking of the text as either literary or informational, efferent or aesthetic, we should think of it as written for a particular predominant attitude or stance, efferent or aesthetic, on the part of the reader. (Rosenblatt 1991a, 445)

Hence, any text can be read aesthetically or efferently, depending of the purpose of the reader. To illustrate, Spink (1996) describes the excitement that his young son exhibited when given a baby hamster, noting how the youngster shuttled back and forth on the reader response continuum as he read and listened to hamster books. At times, his son adopted an efferent stance, absorbing information about how to care for his hamster. At other times, his emotional response was strong, expressing sadness in learning that his hamster would live only two to three years.

While Spink doesn't address nonfiction author studies per se, he is convinced that Rosenblatt's (1978) reader response theory is where we need to begin nonfiction book conversations. It is not hard to extrapolate that Spink would support nonfiction author studies that prioritize the emotional connections that children make to the literature of fact.

> Likewise, science and history, no matter how prosaically expressed, have an inherent potential to capture our imagination because of our human capacity to wonder about our physical universe and our human history. And it is because of, not in spite of, our personal interest and emotional involvement with the topic of study and concomitant texts that learning experience becomes successful and memorable. (1996, 145)

Unlike Mr. Van Loan or Ms. Valanzola, Ms. Chambliss believes that an author study begins and ends with the reader. Accordingly, she solicits personal responses through the use of the arts, drama, discussion, and journal entries as her third graders journey through Cole's works. Influenced by Rosenblatt (1978), she launches and sustains her author study by privileging the reader over the author and the text. However, having honored the "direct experience of literature," Ms. Chambliss doesn't attend to the "study of literature," thereby short-circuiting the literary and literacy understandings that would emerge with the pursuit of biographical and text-based response. As Rosenblatt reminds us: "Once the aesthetic reading of the text has been honored, it might be entirely appropriate to discuss the new information received through the experience" (1991b, 122).

To conclude, each of these perspectives has a rich tradition in the field of literary theory and criticism. While these literary theories have centered on works of fiction, it is fascinating to note advocacy of each of these varying perspectives by present-day nonfiction literacy experts. However, while each has much to offer, no one perspective captures the expansiveness of the literary experience. Thus, I advocate the model of *author study as multiple response* (Jenkins 1999) that merges these three perspectives and acknowledges the continual interplay of aesthetic, text-based, and biographical thought. We turn now to the principles that anchor nonfiction author study as multiple response.

Nonfiction Author Study as Multiple Response: Guiding Principles

Readers Respond in Multiple Ways to an Author's Works

Nonfiction literature has the power to invoke as expansive a range of response as fiction (Gay 2004; McCullough 2001; Weidensaul 2004; Zane 2004). Effective teachers respect the multiplicity of response that readers bring to nonfiction and, by extension, to a nonfiction author study. That said, we must recognize that we prioritize one kind of response over another by the kinds of questions we ask and the comments we make. Pivotal, then, is question of *which* dimension—aesthetic, textual, biographical—receives attention *when* during the author study.

Personal Response to Nonfiction Should Precede Other Types of Response

As has been illuminated in the earlier critiques of the three teachers' approaches to implementing a Joanna Cole author study, I believe that Rosenblatt is right when she argues:

> We peel off layer after layer of concerns brought to bear [in encounters with the text]—social, biographical, historical, linguistic, textual—and at the center we find the inescapable transactional events between readers and texts. (1978, 175)

Teachers who have launched literature-based animal studies of any kind know the levels of exhilaration and wonderment that children bring to such study (Duthie 1996; Jenkins 1999; Roop 1992; Spink 1996). Merely placing an overhead of a shark on a projector or holding up a book on dinosaurs is often enough to incite animated conversation. Effective teachers mine this outpouring of affective response because it serves to ignite and sustain intrigue and interest as well as to tap prior knowledge. Once personal response has been encouraged, children are ready to adopt the stance of literary critic with skillful guidance, examining the text-based, biographical, and other dimensions of literature. Response to nonfiction literature should move from the aesthetic or personal to the efferent (Rosenblatt 1978) whenever possible.

Nonfiction Text Analysis Deepens and Extends Literacy and Literary Development

Ample research has documented that children who have sustained and interactive engagement with fictional literature experience greater success in learning to read and write than do children without a history of book immersion (see synthesis in Snow, Burns, and Griffin 1998). Because the call for immersion in nonfiction literature has only recently been sounded, the research on its benefits is still in its infancy. Not surprisingly, though, comparable findings are beginning to emerge. Children who are immersed in nonfiction literature possess larger vocabularies, use more complex syntax, write in a range of nonfiction genres, and develop an abiding interest in nonfiction literature, to name a few (Caswell and Duke 1998; Duke and Kays 1998; Kamberelis and Bovino 1999; Pappas 1993). In addition, students who are knowledgeable about the following expository text structures comprehend and recall significantly more information (Meyer, Brandt, and Bluth 1980; McGee 1982; Taylor and Beach 1984):

- Description: a text structure that includes information about the characteristics of a topic (person, event, idea) and that employs signal words (also called connectives) such as *for example, in fact, characteristics are,* and *most important*

- Sequence: a text structure in which events, ideas, or steps are logically and sequentially ordered and that uses signal words such as *first, then, finally, before,* and *after*

- Compare and contrast: a text structure that details how two or more things are alike and/or unlike and that uses signal words such as *alike, similar, different, in contrast,* and *however*

- Cause and effect: a text structure that explains how events (effects) occur because of other events (causes) and that employs signal words such as *because, therefore, if . . . then, thus,* and *as a result*

- Problem and solution: a text structure that describes a problem and offers possible solutions and that employs signal words such as *problem, question, solution, solved, answer,* and *if . . . then.*

Research also has shown that instruction in text structures increased both comprehension and composition (McGee 1982; Taylor and Beach 1984; Raphael, Englert, and Kirschner 1989).

After personal response has been entertained, it is important to help children successfully navigate the text. Examples of text-based instruction abound in the chapters of this book. In addition, excellent resources on teaching nonfiction literacy can be found in Buss and Karnowski's (2002) *Reading and Writing Nonfiction Genres;* Duke and Bennett-Armistead's (2003) *Reading and Writing Informational Text in the Primary Grades;* Fountas and Pinnell's (2001) *Guiding Readers and Writers: Grades 3–6;* Harvey's (1998) *Nonfiction Matters;* Portalupi and Fletcher's (2001) *Nonfiction Craft Lessons;* and Robb's (2004) *Nonfiction Writing.*

Biographical Response Heightens the Literary Experience

Author as Person

Recall the opening scenario at the beginning of this chapter in which Mr. Van Loan allows Joanna Cole's autobiography to drive his author study. Each of Cole's works is preceded by autobiographical information; the children then assume the role of detectives, combing the works for biographical links. In my observations of and conversations with teachers, this approach—author study as biography—is by far the most popular. As this chapter has emphasized, though, launching an author study with a full-blown biographical account may compromise readers' personal encounters with the literature by turning the reading experience into a search-and-find mission.

As will be demonstrated in the author studies throughout this book, when children first come to know and appreciate an author's works, they show a greater readiness and curiosity to know the author. While an introduction to the author at the beginning of an author study is important, we should delay the in-depth study of the author until readers have explored some of the author's literature. For it is during this exploration that thoughts about the author begin to percolate. If we encourage students to speculate about the author's life, record their hunches, and, at a later point in the author study, confirm, modify, or revise these biographical speculations, we increase their fascination with this author as well as the degree to which they internalize this biographical information.

Author as Writer

Biographical response includes not only an author's life experiences, dreams, and motivations but also his writing process. Where does she get her ideas? What research techniques does he use? What matters to her? How does he organize his work? Central to this investigation is the construct of intertextuality, the essence of which is cogently captured by Jane Yolen:

> Stories lean on stories, art on art. And we who are the tellers and the artists do what has been done for all the centuries of tellings: We thieve (or more politely borrow) and then we make it our own. (1991, 147)

Intertextuality focuses on the connections that readers and writers forge as they move from one text to another, with *text* defined as any sign (literature, television, film, dance, art, a road sign, a smile) used in social interactions (Short 1992). At the crux of this phenomenon of literary "thieving" is the contention that there is no such thing as an original work and that every text written is tied to other texts (Bakhtin 1986). Writers absorb a world of ideas—historical, social, and political— from their social milieus as well as ways of knowing, and then reiterate, modify, extend, oppose, and/or reenvision these ideas in order to craft their own texts (Bakhtin 1986).

Curious as to the range of intertextual links that children forge when they are immersed in and choose to write nonfiction, a colleague and I (Jenkins and Earle 2006) interviewed eighteen third graders about reports they had written during writing workshop in order to ascertain (a) thematic origins (e.g., "Where did you get the idea to write about . . . ?"), (b) organizational origins (e.g., "Where did you get the idea to organize your report this way?"), and (c) orientational intertextuality (e.g., for each sentence in the report, the third grader was asked, "Where did you learn that information?"). As the third graders mentioned source material(s) in response to these questions, they were asked to retrieve them and locate the information. Analyses of these thematic, orientational, and organizational patterns (Lemke 1992) revealed that the third graders demonstrated multifaceted intertextual knowledge about report writing (Jenkins and Earle 2006). Children, like adults, dip into a vast and varied well of texts when they construct nonfiction pieces, drawing on multiple thematic sources such as books, people, media, and curriculum. Many accessed multiple sources and appropriated the top-level structures of these texts to write their own multichapter reports. In addition, they readily acknowledged the voices that they appropriated. Although the expectation was that the direct quote would constitute the most popular form of appropriation, it ranked behind the paraphrase and the partial direct quote. Not surprisingly, though, their understandings across many of these facets were incomplete, suggesting the need for responsive instruction that would scaffold what they knew with developmentally appropriate insights and strategies.

As the following chapters demonstrate, our instruction should make public the intertextual links that authors such as Jean Fritz and Gail Gibbons employed while writing their nonfiction books. It should show how authors cast wide their nets for ideas, explore how and why authors organize their texts the way they do, and demonstrate how polyphonic voices (e.g., direct quotes, paraphrases, and stylizations—statements of dramatic effect or opinion) infiltrate every act of writing.

Designing a Nonfiction Author Study

Choosing a Nonfiction Author

The selection of a nonfiction author hinges on the quality of her nonfiction literature, on the availability of autobiographical and biographical sources, and, ideally, on the interests of the children and the teacher. In this age of mandated state standards and curriculum frameworks, however, we often have to work to merge interests with curricular priorities.

Whether you or the children choose the author, it is important that the corpus of work meets the standards of quality nonfiction (Figure 1–1). A great nonfiction book evokes a range of aesthetic and intellectual responses if it is "well written, beautifully illustrated, imaginatively laid out, as well as up-to-date, accurate, and thought-provoking" (Russell 1991, 138–39). Choose authors who have a gift for stimulating curiosity, fostering a spirit of inquiry, using eloquent language, and satisfying our need to know and to care.

Recording Multiple Responses to the Author's Nonfiction Literature

Having selected an author, we should consider reading an author's books (or a sampling) in their order of publication to "see the work as a whole, see the development, the evolution of ideas and themes" (Avi 1991, 3). While Avi, Newbery award–winning author, was referring to works of fiction, I heeded his advice when I set out to investigate Joanna Cole's body of work (Jenkins 1999). Because Cole's books exceeded sixty at the time, I selected a representative sample: her earliest works; two books from her Body series (e.g., A Snake's Body [1981]); a few from her birthing series (e.g., A Chick Hatches [1976]); and a handful of her Magic School Bus books.

As I read these works, I recorded personal, text-based, and biographical hunches in a notebook. I recorded these observations not with the intention of sharing each and every one with the children, but rather with intention of targeting teaching possibilities and of ensuring a readiness to acknowledge similar observations that they might offer. An effective author study is not about pursuing every personal response, teaching every literary dimension of the author's craft, or speculating on every possible biographical hunch. Rather, it is about keeping the literature and the author alive by following the children's leads, when possible, with respect to this range of multiple responses.

Criteria for Quality Nonfiction

Accuracy
The content of a nonfiction book must be accurate and up-to-date. Accuracy hinges on the author's expertise. Because many children's nonfiction authors are not for example, scientists or historians, they should provide documentation that their works have been reviewed by experts.

Writing Style
In the words of Russell Freedman, award-winning nonfiction author:

> Certainly the basic purpose of nonfiction is to inform, to instruct and hopefully to enlighten. But that's not enough. An effective nonfiction book must animate its subject, infuse it with life. It must create a vivid and believable world that the reader will enter willingly and leave only with reluctance. A good nonfiction book should be a pleasure to read. It should be just as compelling as a good story. The task of nonfiction is to find the story—the narrative line—that exists in nearly every subject. (1992, 3)

Eloquent, vivid language, passionate intrigue about the topic, and attentiveness to the reader are the staples of nonfiction writing.

Organization
In writing nonfiction, authors sometimes employ one of five organizational structures: description; compare and contrast; sequence; cause and effect; problem and solution (Meyer 1975). A book comparing alligators and crocodiles requires a compare-and-contrast organizational framework; a book about the birth and development of a chick utilizes a sequence structure. Many books, though, necessitate multiple text structures. In addition, readability is often enhanced with inclusion of headings and subheadings as well as with access aids such as tables of contents, indexes, glossaries, and bibliographies.

Visual Displays
Photographs, illustrations, diagrams, maps, and tables work hand in hand with the author's words to stimulate curiosity and to ignite the imagination. The author's ability to harmonize images and words, along with the quality and quantity of these visuals, affects the totality of the work.

FIGURE 1–1   *Adaptation of Huck, Hepler and Hickman's (1987) criteria for quality nonfiction*

To illustrate, I read Cole's first book, *Cockroaches* (1971), and, under aesthetic response, I recorded my first experience with cockroaches in an apartment in Australia that left me sleepless the first two nights and light-drenched from that point on. Under text analysis, I noted Cole's decisions to

- organize information under headings, some humorous and some in question format, such as "The Roach's Relatives" and "Why Have Roaches Survived?"
- present content in a clear, logical fashion, integrating fascinating science and social science facts throughout (e.g., "A hungry cockroach even eats people's fingernails and eyebrows when they are asleep, as sailors on infested ships have found out" [27])
- foreshadow the Magic School Bus series in her conclusion with a cartoon about a woman attacking a cockroach, speech bubble and all.

Having savored a sampling of Cole's works, I was ready to learn about the person behind the pages.

Researching Biographical Links

Note that the search for information about the author follows, rather than precedes, the investigation of the author's books. As readers, we too are entitled to fall captive to the author, to experience the range of affective and cognitive responses to the works, to appreciate the author's craft, and so forth. While the preponderance of autobiographical and biographical information ties to fiction authors, there is increasing interest in the lives of nonfiction writers (Jenkins 1999; Robb 2004).

Print Resources

Autobiographies or autobiographical articles provide a rich source of information. However, autobiographies of nonfiction writers, such as *On the Bus with Joanna Cole* (Cole 1996), Jean Fritz's (1982) *Homesick: My Own Story,* and Milton Meltzer's (1988) *Starting from Home* are the exception, rather than the norm. Notable, however, is the Meet the Author series, published by Richard C. Owen, which offers autobiographies written for young readers by authors such as Lois Ehlert, Jean Fritz, Ruth Heller, Lawrence Pringle, and Seymour Simon.

An excellent resource with respect to both autobiographical and literary qualities of an author's works is the reference book *Children's Literature Review* (Gale Research Co.). In addition to presenting a full biography of and commentary by the author, *Children's Literature Review* offers a compilation of critics' reviews of the author's works. Something About the Author Autobiography Series and *Major Authors and Illustrators for Children and Young Adults* (Gale Research Co.) also contain personal data about family members, a career overview, a listing of the author's books, awards won, and a biographical piece that includes direct quotes from the author. In addition, author profiles can be found in journals such as *Journal of Children's Literature, The New Advocate, Book Links, The Reading Teacher,* and *Language Arts.*

Electronic Resources

Of course, the reigning research tool for biographical information is the Internet. Particularly valuable are the web sites written by the authors themselves (often written for children) as well as those that post interviews with a nonfiction author. Consider the following websites as you begin your pursuit of a particular author:

- The Scoop (Interviews of Authors and Illustrators) http://friend.ly.net/users/jorban/main.html
- Children's Author Websites: www.park-ridge.il.us/library/cdauthors
- Kay Vandergrift's Learning about the Author and Illustrator Pages http://www.scils.rutgers.edu/~kvander/AuthorSite/index.html
- Carol Hurst's Children's Literature Site: www.carolhurst.com
- Yahooligans! http://search.yahooligans.yahoo.com/search/ligans?p=authors and http://yahooligans.yahoo.com/School_Bell/Language_Arts/Authors/

Because websites vary in quality, substance, and authenticity, it is important to learn to successfully navigate the Internet. In Appendix C, coeditor and technology expert Deborah White offers sage advice to help teachers access reputable sites.

Nonfiction Author Studies in Action

In the chapters that follow, the authors present the nonfiction author studies they have designed and implemented in their classrooms. In accordance with the key principles presented in this chapter, each teacher implements curricular events that invite a multiplicity of response. As nonfiction books are introduced and discussed, children are encouraged to share their thoughts, experiences, and feelings with the goals of generating excitement and stimulating curiosity. Inevitably, prior knowledge about the book topic as well as thoughts and questions about the author surface during time set aside for personal response. Because readers and listeners respond to literature in multiple ways, their teachers are not surprised. They acknowledge these text-based and/or biographical comments and promise to return to them in more depth at a later point. After generating personal responses, the teachers formally probe background knowledge, using anticipation guides, Venn diagrams, KWLs, and the like, in order to promote active comprehension. Text analysis then ensues as teachers use the high-quality nonfiction literature to introduce their children to the forms and functions of particular nonfiction genres. Working to meet specific standards stipulated in the *Massachusetts English Language Arts Curriculum Framework*, the teachers provide research-based instruction in particular text structures (e.g., compare and contrast; sequence) or text features (e.g., table of contents, index) or skills (e.g., main idea and details, fact and opinion) appropriate to their grade level. Intertextual connections anchor this instruction: "Let's look at how Gail Gibbons organized her steps for carving a pumpkin. How did she arrange these steps? Why? What time-order words did she use?" Whenever possible, instruction results in an authentic endeavor; application of what has been learned blossoms in an oral or written product (e.g., an animal report that is part of a class PowerPoint presentation to be shared at an assembly; a book talk; a country report; an author biography; a student-generated anticipation guide to be completed by peers). Throughout the instructional sequence, questions and comments about the author undoubtedly emerge. The teachers post these speculations with a promise to share (or to ask the students to investigate) biographical information. Biographical response usually occurs at the midpoint or beyond of the author study. While a brief introduction to the author launches the author study, extended study of life-literature connections and insights into the author's writing process occur after the children have had time to savor some of the author's work, to come to know him first through the work. Finally, to bring each author study to a fitting close, the teachers orchestrate a grand finale. Culminating projects range, for example, from country books on students native homelands to an assembly in which first graders perform a butterfly play and show a PowerPoint presentation of their animal reports, to a videotape of third graders reading segments of their nonfiction reports that was mailed to Jim Arnosky in appreciation for his book *Arnosky's Ark* (1999), who in return sent a letter to the class.

We turn now to these exemplary nonfiction author studies that span the elementary grade levels and include children who have special learning needs and are English language learners. Some of these author studies have been taught repeatedly and represent a synthesis of best curricular events; others have been implemented once and include revisions that would be implemented a second time around. The essential questions, major curricular events, and corresponding local and national standards for each author study are presented in curriculum maps (Jacob 1997) in Appendix A. Each author study is a tribute to the intellectual energy and pedagogical knowledge of its creator and a testimony to the huge payoff for its recipients in terms of nonfiction literacy development.

2

Growing with Gail Gibbons
Grade 1

Peter Niemi and Rosalie Luddy-Lewis

This author study begins on a fall day with a book and an apple tree. We gather our first graders under the apple tree in the school courtyard, show the cover of *The Seasons of Arnold's Apple Tree* (Gibbons 1984), and ask them to help us read the title and to predict the book's content. We then conduct a picture walk through the book, reinforcing the concept of each season. When we arrive at the fall section, we ask the name of the current season and then read the text, hoping that someone will note the discrepancy between Arnold's apple tree, which "now has big, red tasty apples" (unnumbered), and the defoliated, appleless tree under which we sit. Our first graders do not disappoint.

> BRANDI: Apples? What apples? I think this tree is dead.
> KYLE: Somebody must have picked the apples. I wonder where they put them all?
> OLIVIA: My dad thinks the caterpillars ate everything up. They were on everything this year.

The discussion continues about what they think happened to the tree. After tapping and extending their prior knowledge about the town's recent infestation of tent caterpillars, we discuss what the class might do to help this tree. For example:

> BRENT: We need help from a tree doctor, but I don't know one. Does anybody know one?
> LINDSEY: Oh, yeah. We had to spray everything near our house to keep the bugs from eating it all up.

We decide to write a letter to our principal to ask if he can help us save the tree. To ensure that we know how apple trees should look in the full and how they grow throughout the year, we do a read- and think-aloud of *The Seasons of Arnold's Apple Tree*, encouraging text-to-self connections as we go:

> MEGAN: Once I tried to eat the apples when they were starting to grow. My mother told me not to, but I ate them anyway. I got a bad tummy ache.
> MATTHEW: I climbed this huge ladder to pick the best apples on the tree. My mother went nuts. She thought I would fall but I didn't.

During shared writing the next day, the students help us compose the following letter to our principal:

> We need your help! Our apple trees should have apples in the fall, but they don't! They need spraying (to kill the tent caterpillars), fertilizing, and pruning to grow apples. Can you please help us take care of our trees? Many classrooms at the Conley School study about apples in the fall. Our classroom will be studying about apples and apple trees throughout this year. Please help us save the school's apple trees so that we can enjoy them in the future. Can you think about this problem and let us know?
>
> Your friends,
> 1A Yu-Gi-Ohs

With the signature of each first grader attached, we deliver the letter to the principal. The children are happy to learn the following day that their request will be granted.

After a reread of *The Seasons of Arnold's Apple Tree* on a subsequent day, we introduce the concept of sequence by asking them to unscramble pictures of the four stages of an apple, beginning in the spring and ending in the winter. In discussing the sequence, we use time-order words such as *first, then, next,* and *finally,* emphasizing the fixed nature of the tree's growing cycle. To concretize this concept, we have our first graders begin individual journals, recording their observations of the school apple tree in late autumn and then for each additional season during the school year. Prior to each entry, we gather at our apple tree to share our observations and recall information learned from Gibbons' apple books. Students then record their entries individually back in the classroom. Figure 2–1 shows the development of Megan's observing and composing skills. Her ability to detail her scientific observations and to synchronize her illustrations with these observations increases across time. Megan's May and June entries include not only content-rich descriptions but also her attempt to apply what she has been learning about the time-order words that characterize the text structure of sequence (described later; see page 29). These entries remind us how complex these concepts can be to internalize and how our future instruction will need to extend students' understanding of time-order words.

Having responded in multiple ways to one of Gibbons' books, the children are ready to formally meet this author. We hold up the familiar *Seasons of Arnold's Apple Tree* and introduce *Apples* (Gibbons 2000) and ask the children to read the author's

Fall
There is practic ally no
leaves on the tree.
and there is snow all
around the tree.

1

In the winter our
apple tree has no
apples on the

2a

tree.
The tree is bare.
Snow is on the
ground.
(no leaves)
Tiny buds ar on
the branches.
Megan

2b

Our tree is bare,
snow is on the grass and
litlered buds are on each
branch of our tree.

3

(continued)

FIGURE 2–1 *Megan's apple tree journal*

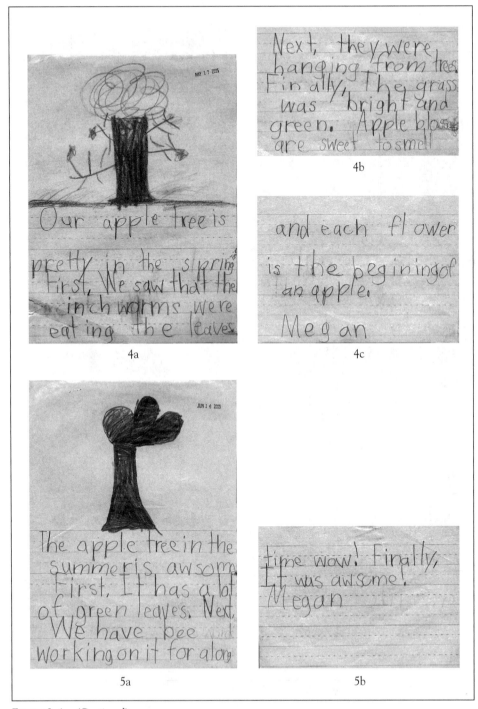

4a

Our apple tree is pretty in the spring. First, We saw that the inch worms were eating the leaves

4b

Next, they were hanging from trees. Finally, The grass was bright and green. Apple blossoms are sweet to smell

4c

and each flower is the begining of an apple.
Megan

5a

The apple tree in the summer is awsome. First, It has a lot of green leaves. Next, We have bee working on it for a long

5b

time wow! Finally, It was awsome!
Megan

FIGURE 2–1 *(Continued)*

name and then to comment on why Gibbons would write two books on apples. Biographical hunches about Gibbons begin.

- Maybe she loves to eat apples.
- I think she remembers picking apples with her family when she was growing up.
- Maybe she likes how things grow and change, like in a garden.

We record their ideas and explain that they will have to do some research to find an answer to our question.

Our author study, originally designed to be completed in eight to ten weeks, extends through the entire school year because of the students' intrigue with Gail Gibbons and her books. This fascination travels from the classroom to home as they borrow books to share with their families. Parents (during open house, conferences, and parent literacy training workshops) tell of interest and excitement beyond the school day.

Our Classroom

As a reading specialist (Peter) and classroom teacher (Rosalie), we coteach a heterogeneous mix of first graders, including learning-disabled, behaviorally challenged, and academically talented students as well as students within the average range, all from lower-middle-class families. The literacy program at our school employs a standards-based, balanced curriculum, with sharing and modeling at the heart of literacy instruction. Peter coteaches daily with each grade 1 teacher for forty minutes of a ninety-minute literacy instructional block. This coteaching focuses on guided reading and writing workshop. Peter also assesses all first graders at regularly scheduled intervals on a benchmark continuum. A library, media, and technology specialist is available for lesson and project support. Students have access to a thirty-station computer lab, equipped with a core projector and a sound system.

Why Gail Gibbons?

Our belief that young children need far more exposure to and modeling of nonfiction text than has been the norm led us to search for an author whose collection would hold the interest of our first graders, advance their literacy processes and skills, and support the topics in our curriculum. Gail Gibbons' award-winning books fit the bill. Her books, which investigate a wide variety of topics, appeal to children's curiosity, stimulate questioning, encourage personal connections, and build factual knowledge and vocabulary to support future content area study. Visual access features such as labels, captions, cross sections, diagrams, and charts not only enhance her texts but also support young readers who may not have the automaticity of decoding to gain meaning from text. So, in partnership with Gail Gibbons and her books, which beg to be comprehended and enjoyed, we set out to

- elicit multiple responses to Gibbons' books: personal connections, text analysis, and biographical investigation
- model and build comprehension strategies through read-alouds and think-alouds
- build awareness of nonfiction text features and text structures
- advance knowledge about a range of topics and information (concepts, facts, vocabulary)
- create interest in and motivation to read and write nonfiction text
- explore links to technology
- satisfy our own curiosity.

The intersection of these goals, the curricular events of this author study and the *Massachusetts Curriculum Frameworks* (ELA, science and/or social studies) and *IRA/ NCTE Standards for the English Language Arts* are presented in a curriculum map in Appendix A.

The Gibbons Author Study in Action

To launch this author study, we purchase or borrow nearly every Gail Gibbons book that has been published—a tall order given that she has written in excess of 130 books. We go the extra mile, though, because we want our six-year-olds to begin to experience the sheer number and variety of books. Before school, we spread the books out on the large classroom meeting rug. Their amazement as they enter the room confirms our instincts:

BRANDI: Look at all these books by this author!
NICHOLAS: It looks like she wrote about everything!
JASON: Wow! Look at all the animal books!

As the first-graders settle down, we assign each table group to a book pile and ask them to sort the books into categories of their own determination. After fifteen minutes, we record and discuss their categories (e.g., animals, sports, space) using a spider web. Students then count the books in each category and construct a bar graph of the results. The students are hooked!

During the categorizing activity, questions about the author emerge. We ask what the children think they know about Gail Gibbons by looking at her books. They are sure she loves animals, eats apples, and likes to write books. We explain that one way we can find out is to read her website. We move to the computer lab and instruct our first graders to enter the URL www.gailgibbons.com, and take a look at Gibbons' website written for children. From the opening page with a picture of her dog saying, "Click here for new pictures from me—Wilson!" to her ads for maple syrup, Gibbons has won over the hearts of our first graders. Continuous talk and conversation can be heard:

MEGAN: So that's what she really looks like. She looks just like my aunt.
THOMAS: She has pets. It looks like a dog and a cat.
CANDACE: Look, there's maple syrup. Does she like it that much?

We walk them through the site, reading aloud text and captions, and encouraging comments and questions:

RYAN: I wonder if she still works on TV shows?
BRENT: I bet she'll write a book on making maple syrup.
SAMANTHA: I want to buy one of her drawings for my grammy. She loves sea birds.

Each student receives a printout of the site to bring home to review and share with her parents. Parents are anticipating this author study, having been informed during parent conferences and through newsletters. We ask the students to think about what they learned about Gail Gibbons, and to be prepared to share their discoveries. The next day we record responses on a biographical web (e.g., "Gail Gibbons even wrote books when she was kid," "She makes maple syrup and sells it so she can make money for charities," and "She went to the rain forest"). The author becomes a real person with interests, feelings, and experiences similar to many in the class. We explain that as we continue to read her books, we will predict other ideas about Gail Gibbons as a person and as a writer and try to verify our speculations.

Having introduced our author, we sustain our first graders' interest by asking them to choose the read-alouds across the school year. Not surprisingly, they choose to follow Gibbons' apple books with *The Pumpkin Book* (1999). Because it is not possible to include all of our lessons in this chapter, we've chosen to profile curricular events of particular books in subsequent sections. Regardless of the book, though, a range of comprehension strategies anchored each of our interactive read-alouds. In the section that follows, we use *Frogs* (1993), one of the many Gibbons books we read in the second half of the school year, to illustrate how we implemented read-alouds and think-alouds, continuously modeling strategies for comprehending nonfiction text in order to promote active thinking and information processing.

Toward an Active Process of Comprehension

Central to effective comprehension is the concept of thinking about thinking—metacognition. I (Peter) explain this concept to the students as the *Little Me*, who sits on my shoulder and asks questions such as: Do I already know something about this topic? Do I understand what is being read? Has it ever happened to me? Am I wondering about what I've heard? During discussions, we use the word *metacognition* and expect students to do the same. The introductory example of the *Little Me* evolves into our *thinking voice inside us.*

Over time, the first graders internalize what good readers do when reading a Gail Gibbons book. For example, Megan, in reference to *Frogs*, explains:

> They [good readers] think in their heads and talk inside about what they are reading. Do they know what Gail Gibbons is telling them? Do they have any questions? They don't just sit there and daydream.

Of course, we realize that Megan's astute response does not mean that she fully comprehends or can actively apply these strategies. Therefore, for the entire year, we model, model, model to make the thinking behind the strategies explicit and clear. This modeling is organized into a before-, during-, and after-reading format to *chunk* the active processing that students should be doing while reading nonfiction text. In the following sections, we illustrate the strategies (Bamford and Kristo 1998; Harvey 1998, 2000) we use before, during, and after a read-aloud of Gibbons' *Frogs* (1993) as well as the array of multiple responses.

To implement the before, during, and after model thoroughly, we explore each new book for approximately five days, for twenty to thirty minutes each day. We find that reviewing what we accomplished the day before helps students assimilate the wholeness of this model. Ownership of this text-processing model is the key to independence in comprehending nonfiction text.

Before Reading

- Set the purposes for both students' reading and the author's writing ("Why am I reading this book? Why do you think Gail Gibbons wrote this book on frogs?"). We develop a common purpose for exploring *Frogs*: learning about the life of a frog and understanding why and how Gail Gibbons writes about this topic.

- Make personal connections. Personal response heightens interest in a topic and often triggers prior knowledge (e.g., "I caught two frogs last summer and they could jump so far that one got away," or "My brother and I used to catch tadpoles in the swamp behind our house.").

- Activate prior knowledge ("What schema do I already have in the filing cabinet in my head about this topic?"). To help the students grasp the concept of prior knowledge, we use the analogy of a filing cabinet, where they open the drawer in their head to check to see if any facts or ideas are inside. Through hand movements, students pretend to pull open the drawer in their head to check for files. Before beginning the book, we tell them that we want them to check their personal filing cabinet on frogs and to share their knowledge via KWLs (what I *know*, what I *want to know*, what I have *learned*), anticipation guides, semantic maps, "I wonder" questions, and so forth. We then model self checking by circling accurate information and making inaccurate information true.

- Preview the book to notice pictures, illustrations, photographs, charts, graphs, labels, diagrams, headings, captions, table of contents, glossary, index, boldface print, and so on. ("What are some things Gail Gibbons has included to show me what she is trying to tell? Can these help my thinking?"). Expect the interplay of personal, literary, and biographical responses to occur during this process. Direct attention to one prominent text feature, such as the labels of the frog body parts, and ask why they think Gail Gibbons includes this text feature.

- Encourage connections to books or media and/or to the world. ("We just heard *The Frog Prince* [Tarcov 1974] and *Froggy Goes to School* [London, 1996]"; "I just took a book out of the library on poison dart frogs"; "My brother and I watched this awesome video on frogs last week on the Discovery Channel.")

- Elicit questions about what is noticed during this browsing. ("What are all those round bubble things?" "Do some frogs stay as tadpoles?" "What's the biggest frog there is? Could it eat my baby brother?" "Can all frogs sing?" "Are frogs like snakes?")

- Expect that the children's insights and knowledge will dictate the course of this before-reading activity; follow their lead when appropriate.

Many of these guidelines also apply to during and after reading. For example, we chart our "I wonder" questions before, during, and after reading ("I wonder how big frogs grow to be?" "I wonder why Gail Gibbons decided to write about frogs?" "I wonder if there will still be frogs in the world when I get to high school?").

During Reading

- Continue to ask questions and make connections. This requires time for talk and sharing. To address time constraints, we adopt the strategy of *turn and talk*. Students choose a neighbor and share questions and connections for two to three minutes. The rules for talking and ending the talking are established and practiced throughout the year: Pick a person next to you for a partner. Talk in a six-inch voice to your partner—ask questions or give information. Be a good listener. Look up to give a signal that you have finished sharing. Everyone stops sharing when he hears the clapping signal. One person from each duo may be asked to share questions or information that you talked about.

- Periodically summarize and reflect on what has been read to that point. ("What we've seen and heard so far is that frog spawn grows into frog embryos, and they then develop into tadpoles. The tadpoles become froglike as their tails shrink and their mouths, gills, and legs change.") Barreling on through the text results in limited comprehension. Our *stop and reflect* times make explicit that good readers stop to do even more thinking about what they are reading. And what if they find what they are reading makes no sense? We model *fix-up* strategies such as rereading, checking picture (visual) clues, using context, and asking for help (Fountas and Pinnell 1996). During our read-aloud of *Frogs*, I purposely make errors to see if students' thinking is engaged. I no sooner get the words out of my mouth when four hands shoot up from students eager to correct me. Samantha explains that what I have just read makes no sense and confuses her. When asked about what could be done now, the students quickly suggest: Reread that part. Let's see the pictures on those two pages again. Go back over the page before that one. Read the last sentence again so we can think more about the word vegetarian." From their suggestions, I realize they are beginning to think strategically.

- Ask them to make predictions and inferences. ("What do you think is going to happen next to the tadpoles? Now that you've heard that people harm frogs, what do you think we could do to help? What does that word *herpetologist* mean?")

- Show them how to determine what the most important information is. Gail Gibbons provides a multitude of visual information to help readers settle on the most important ideas and concepts. Headings, labels, charts, diagrams, graphs, font changes, bold face print, colors, pictures, photographs, and captions are among the text features that we search for and discuss (Harvey 2000). For example, students draw their own diagrams and label the most important parts in the metamorphosis of a frog following the shared reading of *Frogs*. (See Figure 2–2.)

- Make *visual* or *sensory* connections. We encourage students to *close their eyes* and try to see a movie or slideshow of what we have read. Can they *see* the mass of frogs' eggs? Can they *hear* the frogs croaking? This sensory connection facilitates understanding and retention of the text.

After Reading

- Engage students in retelling. We show students how to review the text, how to use the text features, text structures, and strategies (focused on *during* the read-aloud) to synthesize important information. As students develop an understanding of how to determine the most important ideas in a text, the retellings evolve into summaries. (We also make a cumulative list of the most meaningful vocabulary following each retelling. For example, this is our vocabulary list from *Frogs*: *spawn, embryos, tadpoles, gills, lungs, vegetarians, bulges, amphibian, cold blooded, transparent, croak, camouflage, hibernation, herpetologist.*) Students make additional links to the modeled texts and to future encounters.

- Revisit purposes for reading and evaluate the book. ("How successful was Gail Gibbons' presentation of information on frogs?" "Did the book give you information you were looking for?" "Would you recommend this book to someone? Why or why not?")

- Make text-to-text connections across books read to this point. We continue to be amazed at how well our students put new information together and make

FIGURE 2–2   *Frog sequence*

sound generalizations. Our prime example is their discovery of animal classification that evolved after encountering Gibbons' *Penguins* (1998) and *Rabbits, Rabbits, and More Rabbits* (2002b). When presented with a new animal, the students were able to classify the animal correctly. ("Let's see . . . penguins have feathers, lay and hatch eggs, take care of their chicks . . . Penguins are *birds!*" "Look at these rabbits. They have fur, have live babies, and feed their babies milk. Rabbits are *mammals*, like us.") They had begun to build a conceptual framework (see Figure 2–3) and use it to think about other animals.

- Revisit the primary and secondary text structures that the author used to organize the book. Show them how to use what Gibbons teaches us about writing nonfiction in their own writing (subsequent sections in this chapter address this important instruction).

In sum, throughout our Gail Gibbons author study, we modeled continuously with ongoing talk and conversation about nonfiction text. We shared our thinking during the reading process and demonstrated the *strategies* good readers use (make connections, ask questions, make inferences, visualize and make sensory connections, determine important facts and concepts, synthesize, and fix up when comprehension breaks down). The explicit modeling during our think-alouds on a wide variety of Gail Gibbons books introduced our students to the active process of *what* to do and *how* to do it and guided them through that process.

We turn now to the two nonfiction text structures with which our young writers experiment: description and sequence. Ongoing analysis of the text structure of description, which began with Gibbons' *Pumpkin Book*, readied them to write their own description reports at the end of the school year. Likewise, the introduction to the text structure of sequence that began in Gibbons' apple books and continued with subsequent books peaked with formal analysis of this text structure in *Frogs*.

Text Analysis of The Pumpkin Book *and Descriptive Writing*

Recall that our first graders unanimously chose *The Pumpkin Book* (1999) in early October, not surprising with Halloween approaching and pumpkins on display in local stores and farm stands. Text-to-self responses filled our conversations—excited talk about costumes, buying and decorating pumpkins, and haunted houses.

To activate prior knowledge, we pass out an anticipation guide for *The Pumpkin Book* that includes items such as:

Pumpkins are fruits like apples.	T	F
If you want a big pumpkin, you need a big seed.	T	F
It takes 80 to 120 days to grow a pumpkin.	T	F

Before beginning the book, we tell them that we want them to check their personal filing cabinet on pumpkins and use what they know to answer true or false on

Thomas

Descriptive Information	FROG	BALD EAGLE	POLAR BEAR	MONARCH BUTTERFLY
Habitat	swamp pond	near water	Arctic region North Pole	milk weds
Movement	hops swims	flying	wak, runs swim	fly walk
Communication	Croaking	sreech-ing	Growl-ing	with antenn-ae
Outer Covering	moist skin	feather	black skin white fur	scales
Babies/Young	spawn tadpoles	eaglet	1-4 cubs	eggs, chrysalis
Enemies	fish, snake, fox, owls, frogs.	people	humans people	frogs, spider, bird
Diet	frogs insects Plants	fish	Seals, fish, berries	Nectar milk weed
Additional Interesting Facts	they have two lives	egg tooth	Polar bears and pengins never meet	move antennae violently move to mexico

FIGURE 2–3   *Thomas' animal classification*

the anticipation guide. We read each item; they circle true or false. So much discussion erupts as we try to move through the guide that we decide to have the students complete the activity independently while we circulate to clarify confusions and/or assist with difficult words.

We are impressed with the number of times the children reference the items on the anticipation guide during our interactive read-aloud. Because *The Pumpkin Book* is an excellent source for reintroducing the concept of sequence, we focus our discussion during the read-aloud on the growth cycle of the pumpkin from seed to harvest. Without prompting, Kyle draws connections between the growth cycles of apples and pumpkins, allowing us to compare how apples and pumpkins grow. The next day, we revisit *The Pumpkin Book* and extend the concept of sequence to directions, examining in particular how Gibbons sequences the steps in two special entries: "How to Carve a Pumpkin" and "How to Dry Your Pumpkin Seeds." At the end of this session, we readminister the anticipation guide to check understanding; they are pleased with the number of new facts they had gained from the text.

Because *The Pumpkin Book* also contains a good deal of description, and because we need to address a descriptive writing standard in our curriculum frameworks, we focus their attention on descriptive writing. First, we help students notice how Gibbons describes the pumpkins throughout her book. With the class gathered on our meeting rug, we reread passages and discuss descriptors such as *round, tall, small, smooth skin, lots of bumps, prickly vines, small green ball, hard hollow sound, moldy, scary,* and *glowing*. We ask why they think Gail Gibbons uses so many descriptive words. A sample of responses includes the following:

LINDSEY: She wants to help us see a picture in our heads.
BRANDI: To make it interesting and not boring.

We emphasize that good writers, like Gail Gibbons, include descriptive words in their writing to help the reader paint a clear picture in her mind. We then reread a few highly descriptive sentences from *The Pumpkin Book* while asking the students to close their eyes to try to see what is being described. We finish with a quote from Gail Gibbons':

I want to make nonfiction visually exciting, but it's sort of natural for me to do that. I mean I love bright colors, and I love doing my artwork. But when I'm plotting out a book, because of my graphic background and because of the television background, I can sort of visualize while I'm writing what is going to be on each page. And I don't want it to be boring. I want it to be visually exciting. I will never do a topic that is dull or uninteresting. It has to really be something that I want to dig into and be curious about. (Reading Rockets n.d.)

After revisiting Gibbons' pumpkin decorating ideas using paint, glitter, ribbon, and cut paper, we ask our first graders to decorate a pumpkin. We then ask them to write a description of their pumpkin detailed enough that it can be located in the pumpkin patch that we created in one corner of the room. To organize this descriptive writing, we develop the following template for a writing frame: (a) the opening sentence contains a general descriptive statement (e.g., clothing); (b) subsequent sentences describe the hair, eyes, nose, mouth, and size; and (c) the closing sentence is "Can you find my pumpkin?"

They then read their descriptions and go on a pumpkin hunt as we compliment them on their inclusion of key descriptive details. This writing activity engages even our most reluctant of writers. Emily, who does not like putting pen to paper, is quite motivated to have her pumpkin found:

> My pumpkin has a dark green hat with little black spots on it.
> My pumpkin also has yellow hair and some dark green spots.
> She has one black eye and one black eye with an orange circle around it.
> Her nose is a small red triangle.
> Her mouth is a wide green smile.
> Finally, my pumpkin is medium-sized.
> Can you find my pumpkin?

Gibbons' text and the template served as effective scaffolds for our first-grade writers, ensuring the use of descriptive language and purposeful writing.

Gail Gibbons Teaches the Text Structure of Sequence

As previously noted, our first graders had been steeped in the text structure of sequence from the beginning of the year. In *The Seasons of Arnold's Apple Tree*, they were introduced to the fixed order of the seasons and an apple tree's growth. In *The Pumpkin Book*, they revisited the concept of the growth cycle from pumpkin seed to plant, as well as the steps to carving a pumpkin. In *Monarch Butterfly* (1989), students learned the butterfly life cycle stages as well as the sequential journey of butterfly migration. This ongoing immersion in and discussion about the sequence structures found in Gibbons' books readied children for formal instruction on this text structure, which occurred during our study of *Frogs*. An outline of our instructional plan follows:

- Reintroduce the concept of sequence by modeling examples of other things that are sequential: alphabet letters, numbers, days of the week, months of the year, seasons, directions.
- Review the apple tree, pumpkin, and seed-to-plant life cycles in previously read Gail Gibbons books; show parallels.
- During first read-aloud of *Frogs*, explicitly discuss the order of the developing frog; establish the meaning of the word *sequence*; and highlight time-order words.
- Revisit book (second read-aloud), encouraging students to verbalize the fixed order of frog development, using illustrations as possible cues and time-order words.

- Construct a sequence graphic organizer with *Frogs* data (boxes, time line, list form) with the class.
- Have students independently sequence and label four illustrations showing the frog growth sequence (see Figure 2–2).
- Summarize the sequences shared in Gail Gibbons' books to date and develop a gist statement, for example, *A sequence is things happening in a certain order.*

Sequence is one of five prominent text structures found in nonfiction literature. Across this author study, we also discussed the other text structures (e.g., compare and contrast; cause and effect; problem and solution) Gail Gibbons uses to organize the information in her books. While space doesn't permit a discussion of how we introduced each of these structures across the school year, we generally organized our instruction as follows:

- Read aloud the Gail Gibbons book and explicitly explain the specific structure during a think-aloud.
- Using exemplary passages from Gibbons' book, explain how the structure works by constructing a structure-specific graphic organizer.
- Revisit the text and have students explain the structure.
- Review and summarize all connections and links to the specific text structure.
- Develop a gist statement to explain the text structure simply and clearly (e.g., *Compare and contrast means showing how things are the same and how they are different*).

With our guidance, students created *anchor charts* for each text structure using content from one or more of Gibbons' books. For example, first we examined the following passages from Gibbons' *Soaring with the Wind: Bald Eagles*:

Once there were thousands of bald eagles in North America. Then people began hunting them for sport. Farmers shot them because they falsely believed bald eagles killed small farm animals and too many fish. Also, people moved into wilderness areas, cutting down trees and destroying the eagles' territory. (1998, unnumbered)

Then the farmers sprayed their fields with a poison, called DDT, to protect their crops from pests. Rainwater carried the DDT into waterways, poisoning fish and other sources of the bald eagles' food. When eagles fed on prey that was contaminated with DDT, some died. Others laid eggs that never hatched because DDT had made the eggshells so thin and soft. In 1969, only a few hundred pairs of these birds were left in the lower 48 states.

We presented a graphic organizer that was organized as follows: on the right side, under the label "Causes," were four blank boxes; arrows shot from each box to one large box on the left side. We asked our first graders to help us fill in four causes of the bald eagle's endangerment and then determine the main effect. We used anchor charts to reinforce the concept of each text structure as we encountered it in a new book. Although this seems to be a high-level thought process, the students were able to make structure connections easily when guided by their anchor charts. As Kyle and Matthew remarked during the discussion of a new book, *Chicks and Chickens* (2003): "This describes all different kinds of chickens and this part tells about the sequence of an egg hatching. And this part compares how chickens are raised on a small farm and on a big farm."

Gail Gibbons as Person and Writer

As previously mentioned, short of an author visit, the Internet was the best way to bring Gail Gibbons to our classroom. Each time we introduce and share a new Gail Gibbons book, students go online to try to answer questions the new book generates (e.g., "Does Gail Gibbons like to sew quilts?" "What is her favorite sport or sports team?" "What's she going to write about next?"). Students frequently access two additional websites to check biographical information: www.edupaperback.org and barbsbooks.com/gibbons.htm. We also share information learned from multiple sources (see Gail Gibbons' author profile on page 32).

As a biographical summarizer, the class creates an acrostic poem, using Gail Gibbons' name. Prior to writing this acrostic, students had created biographical acrostic poems about themselves, using their first and last names. Thus, they successfully merge biographical data and alphabet knowledge to create the following poem:

Graphic artist	Goose Green Maple Syrup
Asks many questions	Illustrates and sells cards
Illustrator and author	Big book artist
Loves books	Bats, bears, birds
	Oak Park, Illinois, 1944
	Nonfiction books
	Swimming, boating, reading, writing

In addition, to extend their intrigue with Gail Gibbons and to encourage use of technology, students play a *Jeopardy*-based PowerPoint game and an online quiz that we created. Categories for the game are based on Gail Gibbons' books, interests, family, honors, and additional biographical data. During one session of playing the game, Olivia blurts out: "I want to be Gail Gibbons when I grow up!" Another student comments: "This is so cool . . . our own *Jeopardy* game! I think I can answer all the questions about Gail Gibbons' books. We like the same things. It would be awesome meeting her someday. Maybe we could show her our *Jeopardy* game?" The PowerPoint quiz, available for both school and home use, contains examples such as:

$300: What is one of the rarest, bamboo-eating animals in the world? Answer: Giant Pandas

$400: As a child, what word would best describe Gail Gibbons? Answer: Curious

Gail Gibbons

Born: August 1, 1944
Careers: cartoonist, illustrator, designer, animator, model builder, commercial and fine art sculptor, author
Awards: More than twenty awards from organizations such as New York City Art Director Club, American Institute of Graphic Arts, National Science Teachers Association, American Library Association, Washington Post Children's Book Award, and the International Reading Association
Home: Corinth, Vermont

Gail Gibbons is the author and illustrator of more than 130 nonfiction children's books. She has enlightened youngsters "about the mysterious workings of clocks and locks, detailed the plethora of trucks and trains in the world, and taken young readers behind the counter of department stores, post offices, and fire departments. Her brightly illustrated books have introduced . . . readers to the world of sharks and sea turtles, and have educated still others to the mechanics of everything from weather to building a skyscraper" (Hedblad 1999, 63).

Gibbons credits her artistic talent to her father, who was awarded an art scholarship to attend Chicago's Art Institute but declined because his parents thought that a career in the arts would be foolhardy. His subsequent career as a tool-and-die designer undoubtedly left its mark on Gibbons; her intrigue with machines and how they work has yielded multiple books. To write *Clocks and How They Go* (1979), Gibbons dismantled the clocks in her house: "I still have two boxes of clock parts left" (Holtz 1988, 97). With an art degree in hand, Gibbons began her career in television, including children's television, doing set design, graphics, and animation. It wasn't long before the lure of writing and illustrating children's books took hold.

Gibbons on Gibbons: Quotes About Her Childhood

On what she was like as a child: I've always loved drawing and painting. I was also a very curious child. My parents tell me that I was always asking lots and lots of questions" (Gibbon 2002, 11).

On books: "At this time I became an avid reader. Each night I would climb in bed with piles of books. When my light was supposed to be out, I would still be reading" (Gibbons 1991, 71).

On the first book she wrote: "At the age of ten, I remember putting my first little book together. I lived in an apartment house that didn't allow pets and I really wanted a pet dog in the worst way. So, I wrote a story about a girl who owned a dog named Flip. It was my first picture book that I ever put together" (Gibbons 1991, 71).

On who inspired her: "He (a college instructor who illustrated children's books) became sort of an idol for me. I couldn't believe that his work was printed into very fine-looking books" (Hedblad 1999, 64).

Gibbons on Gibbons: Quotes About Her Writing Process

On how she got into writing: "I moved to New York City, where I got a job doing artwork for television shows. Eventually I was asked to do the artwork for a children's show. While doing that show, some of the children asked me if I had ever thought of doing children's books. My mind immediately recalled how much I enjoyed doing that as a child. So, I put together an idea for a book and right away a publisher bought it. That book was called *Willy and His Wheel Wagon.* Since then, over 100 books that I have written and illustrated have been published" (Gibbons 2002, 1).

On research: "Nonfiction requires a tremendous amount of research. I want it to be accurate and up-to-date information" (Hedblad 1999, 67). "I go to bookstores and libraries to gather information, but I don't trust books solely, because they can have mistakes. So I find an expert, someone who knows a lot about the subject I'm writing about. That way I'm sure to get the most up-to-date information. I over-research. I always end up with much more information than I can use. I want to be sure I've covered everything. If you notice, in a lot of my books there's a lot of information on page 32. Those are extra things that I found that I think are sort of neat, except I couldn't fit them elsewhere in the book" (Kovacs and Preller 1993, 26–27).

On revision: "It can really be draining at times. Like when you are explaining how a skyscraper is built and you only have 27 pages, three sentences per page. It's watching the pieces of a puzzle finally fitting together. Bit by bit it takes form" (Kovacs and Preller 1993, 27).

On why she loves writing: "I also get to travel and meet lots of interesting people. While doing research for my book *Nature's Green Umbrella: Tropical Rain Forests,* I traveled to two islands where there are tropical rain forests, Saba and Dominica. I had a great time writing and illustrating the book. I get a lot of pleasure from doing the type of work I do" (Gibbons 2002, 1).

Gibbons on Gibbons: Outside Interests

"I have many hobbies, like swimming and boating, but my favorites are reading and creating books" (Gibbons n.d., 2).

Biographical References

Gibbons, G. 1991. "Gail Gibbons." *Something About the Author Autobiography Series.* Detroit: Gale Research.

———. 2002. "Gail Gibbons." Retrieved June 5, 2005 from www.gailgibbons.com.

———. n.d. "Gail Gibbons." Retrieved June 20, 2002 from www.harpercollins.com/catalog/author_xml.asp?authorID=12129.

Hedblad, A. 1999. "Gibbons, Gail." *Something About the Author (Vol. 104).* Detroit: Thomson Gale.

Holtz, S. 1988. *Sixth Book of Junior Authors and Illustrators.* New York: H. W. Wilson.

Kovacs, D., and J. Preller. 1993. *Meet the Authors and Illustrators. Vol. Two.* New York: Scholastic.

Reading Rockets. n.d. Transcript from an interview with Gail Gibbons. Retrieved Oct. 1, 2006 from www.readingrockets.org/books/interviews/gibbons/transcript.

Gail Gibbons Books Used During this Author Study

Gibbons, G. 1979. *Clocks and How They Go.* New York: Crowell.

———. 1984. *The Seasons of Arnold's Apple Tree.* New York: Harcourt Brace.

———. 1989. *Monarch Butterfly.* New York: Holiday House.

———. 1993. *Frogs.* New York: Holiday House.

———. 1994. *Wolves.* New York: Holiday House.

———. 1998. *Penguins.* New York: Holiday House.

———. 1998. *Soaring with the Wind: Bald Eagles.* New York: Morrow Junior.

———. 1999. *The Pumpkin Book.* New York: Holiday House.

———. 2000. *Apples.* New York: Holiday House.

———. 2001a. *Pigs.* New York: Holiday House.

———. 2001b. *Polar Bears.* New York: Holiday House.

———. 2002a. *Giant Pandas.* New York: Holiday House.

———. 2002b. *Rabbits, Rabbits, and More Rabbits.* New York: Holiday House.

———. 2003. *Chicks and Chickens.* New York: Holiday House.

———. 2004. *Thanksgiving.* New York: Holiday House.

———. 2005. *Owls.* New York: Holiday House.

Following Olivia's lead, we ask how many think they could do what Gail Gibbons does and write a report on an animal of their choice. Hands fly and animated talk suggested an endorsement of the report writing project, to which we now turn.

Report Writing/PowerPoint Project and Presentation

In preparation for report writing, we ask our first graders to help us develop an animal web template. Using the organizational scheme of Gail Gibbons' animal books and a kid-friendly research data source called *Animals of the World* (Grolier Educational Corporation 1995), we generate the web in Figure 2–4 using Kidspiration, a beginning word-processing software program. We explicitly model the ways writers locate information, record data, and write paragraphs that use a description text structure. Selecting two animals (sea otter, hippopotamus) from a theme in our reading anthology and with the active support of the media specialist–librarian, the

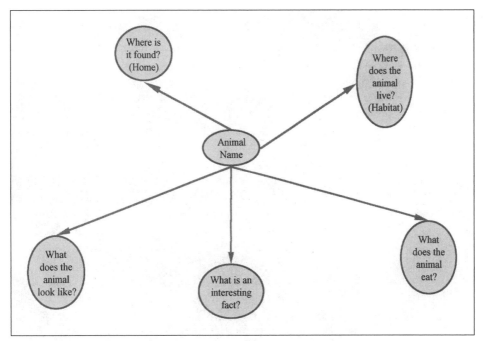

FIGURE 2–4   *Animal web template*

classroom teacher, and the reading specialist, students move through the following research procedure:

- Locate information in magazines, encyclopedias, specific animal books, and on the Internet. (This search [materials preplanned] takes place in the school library.)
- Photocopy or print out sections of information addressing template topics (e.g., habitat, animal features).
- On the copies, highlight specific information to include in the report and write information in appropriate places on the writing (web) template.
- Using the writing template, construct complete sentences, incorporating the animal research information (on the board and chart paper, with the teacher recording).
- Collaborate with teachers to develop introductory and clincher sentences for the report. (We read sample introductory and clincher sentences from Gail Gibbons' paragraphs to model authentic formats for these types of sentences.)
- Reread the completed report, revisiting the animal web categories to see if all have been addressed and to make sure the report aligns with the description text structure.

After modeling the procedure for both the sea otter and the hippopotamus (which required three forty-minute work sessions to complete entire process), we are confident the students are capable of working more independently to complete an animal research report.

In early May, students brainstorm a list of animals that we label: "Amazing Animals of the World." Working in self-selected pairs, each team chooses an animal of interest from the list to research. With the support of the school librarian–media specialist, classroom teacher, and reading specialist (throughout the project), partners actively locate resources, photocopy data, highlight targeted information, and record data on the web template. On another day, the students begin writing their one-paragraph reports about their animals, again using the data template for facts and topic organization. (Partners take turns writing and coaching.) We brainstorm possible topic sentences before writing begins and give students the option of using one of the brainstorms or developing one of their own. Then they write four additional detailed sentences addressing the template topics. We again model paragraph clincher (ending) sentences from several Gail Gibbons books and brainstorm a list of potential formats to be used. Students can (and some do) choose to design their own clincher sentence formats. On a third day, partners coedit their paragraphs. Following this editing, student pairs meet with the district media specialist to create and build two PowerPoint slides about their animal, one for their report and the other for a detailed drawing of the animal. We use the Scholastic Keys program for this independent typing and drawing. The partners take turns with the writer and illustrator jobs. William and Thomas' PowerPoint slides on the Bengal tiger are presented in Figure 2–5.

Our first graders have become authors and illustrators, just like Gail Gibbons! The media specialist burns PowerPoint CDs of the class collection of nonfiction paragraphs and illustrations. With added music and a few eye-catching introductory graphics, the students are almost ready to present their nonfiction masterpiece to their families. With the help of big buddies, aides, volunteers, and specialists, the first graders practice reading their paragraphs with phrasing, fluency, and expression. The PowerPoint presentation for their families, in conjunction with the class play described in the next section, is a true showcase for their learning. These students have become accomplished researchers, writers, and presenters.

Our Class Play

Interweaving factual information from the Gail Gibbons books we have read throughout the year, we (Peter and Rosalie) write a three-act play titled *Betty Butterfly's Welcome Home Party* (see Act 1 in Figure 2–6), as the second part of the culminating activity for our yearlong author study. After introducing our first graders to the play format, we practice reading the play chorally to build fluency with particular attention to phrasing, rate, and expression. We solicit volunteers to play the characters of Betty and Arnold. Because many students want these lead roles, we ask them to practice the parts over the weekend. This is a major undertaking for our students, but we know

Bengal Tiger
by William and Thomas

A Bengal Tiger lives in South East Asia. It lives in forests and on mountains. It looks like a big cat that is up to 10 feet long and can weigh between 400 to 575 pounds. It has black and orange stripes. The Bengal tiger eats deer, pigs, and other forest animals. An interesting fact is some males (boys) occupy a territory of 200 square miles. A second interesting fact is this tiger usually kills its prey by biting its neck or throat.

FIGURE 2–5   *William and Thomas' PowerPoint on the Bengal tiger*

Betty Butterfly's Welcome Home Party

Cast of Characters

Betty Butterfly, Ducks, Bees, Frogs, Rabbits, Hummingbirds, Sparrows, Arnold, Apple Blossoms (3), Milkweeds (2), Eggs

Act 1

Opening Scene: In a garden near Arnold's apple orchard.

ARNOLD: Hey Betty! Is that you?

BETTY: Yeah! It's me. I'm finally home.

SPARROWS: Why were you gone so long?

BETTY: Well Sparrows, every fall I migrate to Mexico where it is warmer and where I can find food to eat. Every spring I return to the apple orchard to lay my eggs.

SPARROWS: Why now, Betty?

BETTY: In the spring the weather is warmer because our part of the Earth starts to tilt towards the sun and everyone knows . . .

ALL: The reason for the seasons is the tilt of the Earth. (*clap*) The reason for the seasons is the tilt of the Earth. (*snap*) The reason for the seasons is the tilt of the Earth. (*clap*)

RABBITS: Did you have an exciting winter in Mexico, Betty?

BETTY: Well . . . You wouldn't believe this! I found this great place to stay. It is called Casita Verde. They had the best flowers. I've never tasted such delicious nectar!

HUMMINGBIRDS: I've stayed there! It is awesome!

BEES: What kind of flowers did you sip?

BETTY: Casita Verde has petunias, roses, and lilies just to name a few.

ARNOLD: The nectar in my apple blossoms is mighty tasty. Why don't you try some?

APPLE BLOSSOMS: Our nectar is divine. It's really, really fine. Come and sample some of mine! It's really, really fine.

BETTY: This is terrific!

RABBITS: Hey Betty, let's go down to the pond to see the ducks.

FIGURE 2–6   *Act 1 of script performed by first graders as a culminating activity*

that with hard work and determination, they can memorize the lines. On Monday, each child auditions for the part he or she wants. Olivia and Kyle are amazing! Everyone agrees that they should be Betty Butterfly and Arnold. The rest of the play parts are handled in the same way. Every child has a part, and several have two. Once all the parts are filled, the scripts become nightly homework, to be read and studied *with* parents. The goal is automaticity with expression and volume in line delivery.

Each student is also responsible in some way for creating the scenery. Megan draws and paints the centerpiece apple tree, while the rest of the class designs, cuts, and pastes apple blossoms on the tree. Samantha and Candace paint, cut, and mount three suns, one for each scene. Everyone works on sky, grass, and clouds. The three different scenes come together quickly. Students are proud to showcase their artistic talents. It is teamwork at its best! The most difficult part of the preparation is designing the costumes. We search for ideas online and download clip art samples. For each costume, we make a transparency and project it on colored construction paper. Students then trace and cut out each; frogs, hummingbirds, sparrows, bees, ducks, rabbits, and milkweeds cover the classroom! Olivia contributes her butterfly wings from a recent dance recital.

The children practice the play daily for two full weeks, with a dress rehearsal performance for the entire first-grade audience. They also practice several fact-based chants (*The reason for the seasons is the tilt of the Earth.*) and a butterfly poem set to music for students to sing. We invite families to attend the command performance on the school stage (see Figure 2–7). Digital and video cameras are everywhere! The kids feel like movie stars. Our library media specialist makes two master videotapes, one for

FIGURE 2–7 *Students perform* Betty Butterfly's Welcome Home Party

our class archives and the other to keep in the library for on-loan viewing by the school community. The students are mesmerized as they view themselves on television.

The strong senses of community, ownership, and pride cultivated by teamwork and cooperation throughout this play preparation and performance show us the potential of this vehicle for expressing aesthetic connections to nonfiction concepts. With the inclusion of poetry, chants, music, and movement, the play also connects with multiple intelligences (Gardner 1993). Overwhelmingly positive feedback from peer, staff, and family audiences end our author study on a high note. The combination of the PowerPoint show and play presentation is a true *celebration* of our yearlong journey through the nonfiction world of Gail Gibbons.

Concluding Comments

During this author study, our first graders were marinated in Gail Gibbons' nonfiction books. Through read-aloud and think-aloud modeling, we helped them practice the comprehending strategies good readers use. They assimilated many new facts, concepts, and vocabulary. They learned to use technology—PowerPoint, Kidspiration, and Scholastic Keys—as a tool to support their literacy learning. They learned how one very accomplished writer goes about her trade, delighting in the knowledge that writers are real people who own dogs, make maple syrup, and have families. And emulating this author, they tried their hand at writing nonfiction.

As we look back on this year, we are taken with the interest and motivation that our first graders showed about reading and writing nonfiction text. Parents told us that their children were constantly asking them to buy nonfiction books. Independent and journal writing about nonfiction topics doubled. Students cited Gail Gibbons' books as some of their favorites. One child said, "My favorite book is *Chick and Chickens* by Gail Gibbons because I never knew how chickens lay and hatch eggs. I want to read her book about seagulls now." Library borrowing of nonfiction books for independent use tripled by June.

We also are taken with how much we have grown as teachers, as kidwatchers. Most striking has been the realization that our students are capable of a much higher level of comprehending and thinking about nonfiction than we thought possible. The following are images and/or results of this higher-level of thinking:

- personal connections to topics, which elicit prior knowledge
- asking deeper questions, searching for answers, considering more than one right answer
- risk taking and stamina: "If I can't find out about bats here, I can go there. I'll keep looking because I *have* to know how many mosquitoes the bats near my house eat."
- Inferencing: "If I know that all mammals have hair, then a whale has to have hair somewhere. I'll look in this book about whales to find out where the hair is."
- Increase in vocabulary (e.g., *migration, metamorphosis, vegetarian*)

We are already planning to conduct another Gail Gibbons author study throughout the next school year, incorporating additional books and maintaining our high expectations for student learning. As we look back, we realize that an author study requires true commitment. It is not something that can be handled superficially. Starting slowly helps, as does selecting read-alouds that you enjoy yourself. Watching and listening to kids' reactions will guide the way. Nonfiction has a way of hooking into their very beings! Conversations, discussions, and interactions promoting *talk, talk, talk* are as essential to a nonfiction author study as they are to all true learning. Children need to share their thoughts, feelings, and understandings, as well as listen to those of others. It's what opens minds to new worlds. It's what a nonfiction author study is all about.

3

On the Go with Ann Morris
Grade 2

Julie Coppola and Joanne George

The books are displayed on the round table below a large world map for all the second graders to see as they first enter Joanne George's classroom. "New books," Eduardo notices right away. "We have new books!" The photographs on the book covers are bright and inviting. It is immediately evident that these photographs mirror the diversity of the ethnic, linguistic, and cultural backgrounds of the children in Joanne's classroom. Some of these children are recent arrivals to the United States and speak little English; others are earlier arrivals and appear confident in their growing abilities to read, write, and speak English. Some were born in the United States but began school with few or no English skills. It seems only fitting that these students, along with their native English–speaking classmates, will be introduced to Ann Morris, an author who has spent much of her writing life traveling and documenting how children and adults throughout the world go about their daily lives.

Harnessing Eduardo's excitement, Joanne introduces *On the Go* (1990), an easy reader about transportation throughout the world. To ensure that all the children will know some transportation vocabulary, Joanne asks them to help her generate a list of ways people travel in the United States, recording their responses on chart paper (see Figure 3–1). Any doubts about the author choice or whether the students will respond personally to this nonfiction book are dispelled as Joanne begins to read aloud. The photographs and the text invite the children to share their experiences of traveling by foot or car or plane or even on a large animal. The first page with the accompanying photograph of a mother carrying her baby in a sling on her back prompts immediate outcries.

"You can do this in Africa!" exclaims Samuel.

"We do that in my country!" Arthur adds.

The picture of people traveling by oxen prompts one child to state emphatically with very wide eyes, "I did that." Joanne wonders aloud where this photograph was taken. She tells the children that to learn this information, the reader must go to the

FIGURE 3–1   *Students brainstorm types of transportation*

index that contains page numbers, a smaller version of each photograph, and more information about each photograph. Joanne selects another photograph and models the steps for using the index. She reads aloud from the index about double-decker buses. Greg comments, "My nana went to England and she saw one, and I went to New York, and I saw one."

Joanne again models locating information in the index. She asks Micah, a boy from Nigeria, to work with her as she locates information about a photograph of a boy riding his bicycle on a dusty path. Micah responds, "That Nigeria. We do that in Nigeria. I have my bike in Nigeria."

Isata reports knowingly, "In Uganda, they didn't have roads. They only had dirt on the ground."

Finally, Joanne shows the children the world map on the last page. She asks Micah to name the continent where they will find Nigeria, and together they locate the country. Angela points out that the map in the book is the same as the large map that Joanne had placed earlier on the bulletin board. Joanne explains that, like Ann Morris, they too will be labeling the world map. Joanne pulls out a photograph of Micah from an envelope filled with photographs that she had taken of each child in preparation for the author study. Together, she and Micah first locate Africa and then place Micah's picture on Nigeria. Over the next few days, as the class discusses the continents during social studies, Joanne will help children first locate and then place their photographs on their countries of origin.

Multiple copies of *On the Go* have been placed at each of the children's tables. Just as Joanne is about to send the children back to their tables to partner read the text and practice using the pictorial index, Maria provides the first biographical response. "Does Ann Morris go to all these places?" she wonders. Joanne tells the children there is no information about Ann Morris in *On the Go*, so they will have to use other resources to learn about the author. Joanne writes Maria's question on a new piece of chart paper, and she tells the children that it is an important question that will have to be answered about Ann Morris.

So begins our author study with twenty-three second graders in an urban school district populated largely by students who speak home languages other than English and who live at or below the poverty level. As a classroom teacher (Joanne) and teacher educator (Julie), we first collaborated as a result of a university-school partnership supported by a Reading First grant. After three years of funding was exhausted, we have continued to work together with the goal of exploring effective literacy instructional practices for students who are learning English as they are learning to read and write. This nonfiction author study represents one of their collaborations. The author study was implemented during a school year in which fifteen students from Brazil, Cambodia, Colombia, Dominican Republic, Kenya, Laos, Nigeria, Philippines, Puerto Rico, Sierra Leone, Thailand, Uganda, and Zimbabwe and seven native English–speaking students made up Joanne's general education classroom.

Thus, our work was shaped by the need to respond to the particular question raised by increasing numbers of general education teachers whose classrooms enroll English language learners (ELLs): How can I meet the literacy learning needs of children who are not yet proficient in the language of instruction? In this chapter, we demonstrate how we responded to this challenge in one classroom with students with varying levels of English proficiency. We begin with a brief overview of effective literacy instructional practices for ELLs. Next, we provide a description of literacy instruction in Joanne's classroom. Then, we demonstrate how a nonfiction author study provided opportunities for multiple response that supported the development of oral language, literacy, and content knowledge among ELLs.

Teaching English Language Learners

Although important questions remain about how children become readers and writers in their second and often weaker language, the evidence suggests the course of development shares more similarities than differences with the stages of first language literacy development (Fitzgerald and Noblitt 1999). This evidence also indicates that promising instructional approaches for ELLs build upon effective approaches for English-only students. Opportunities to tap background knowledge, opportunities to read and write and talk for authentic purposes, explicit vocabulary instruction with particular attention to academic vocabulary, explicit instruction in reading comprehension strategies, a conceptually challenging curriculum that parallels the curriculum presented to their native English–speaking peers (Gersten and Jimenez 1998; Meier 2004) combine to prepare ELLs for success in school. Home-school partnerships that value immigrant families' contributions to their children's education are also essential for academic achievement (Garcia 2005). Similar to their first language counterparts, young second language learners benefit from a systematic, explicit approach to teaching the sound-symbol relationships of their new language (Lesaux and Siegel 2003) and from meaningful word study (see Bear et al. 2003). Consistent opportunities to hear, read, and experiment with writing connected text helps ELLs strengthen these developing understandings about English sounds and letters and spelling patterns as well as vocabulary and syntax. Explicit instruction in English text structures and in the vocabulary and language structures used to organize texts are also necessary for language and literacy development (Wong-Fillmore and Snow 2002). Students' growing abilities in their second language are supported by opportunities to read and reread texts that provide clear models of the vocabulary, syntax, and text structures necessary for participation in ongoing classroom instruction (Lenters 2004–2005). Finally, teachers' careful attention to integrating reading, writing, and oral language instruction leads to growth in language and literacy (Au 1998). In the next section, we provide an overview of literacy instruction in Joanne's classroom.

Our Classroom

The children in Room 18 learn in a print-rich environment with easy access to materials that support developing readers and writers. These include bins of books organized by genre, theme, and level of reading difficulty; children's literature titles and big books prominently displayed on a large bookcase; and an abundance of writing materials housed at the writing center. The children's reading folders, used to organize their reading logs and daily written responses to reading selections, and the children's writing folders that contain a writing piece in progress, are retrieved easily from personalized bins and cubbies that circle the room. Important classroom areas such as the listening center and objects such as tape recorders are labeled. Purposeful wall displays include samples of the children's original work exemplifying each step of the writing process, a word wall, and charts with content vocabulary. Seating and furniture arrangements are flexible, allowing Joanne and the children to transition easily from whole-group to small-group to independent activities. Joanne has set aside one corner of the classroom to accommodate whole-class lessons. Here she stores a large easel, chart paper, and markers for use as she conducts her lessons with the children gathered in front of her on a rug. Joanne pays careful attention to implementing consistent instructional routines, allowing for increased student independence. Joanne also employs consistent language to organize those routines, a practice that is helpful for her ELLs, particularly for those who continue to arrive throughout the school year.

A classroom schedule with daily tasks guides the children through the two to two and a half hours devoted daily to reading and writing instruction. Reading instruction is organized by three main activities: Community Reading, Just Right Reading, and On Your Own Reading (Paratore 2000). Community Reading is the time when Joanne ensures that all students have access to grade-appropriate text. Joanne plans multiple opportunities with differing levels of support for all the children to hear or read and respond to the grade-level anthology. Community Reading is followed by Just Right Reading, when Joanne provides small-group, guided reading instruction that targets students' word-level and comprehension needs. During this time, Joanne selects leveled texts from her classroom library as well as from the schoolwide book room. This is followed by On Your Own Reading, a time when most children self-select texts to read individually or with a partner. Students who need more support are helped to choose a text and often read with the classroom aide. Joanne also reads aloud to the class daily, choosing from a range of children's literature titles. The read-aloud provides another opportunity to introduce the students to a variety of genres, to demonstrate ways to respond to literature, and to point out the language of books.

A half-hour writing block follows reading instruction four days a week (see Coppola et al. 2005 for an extended discussion). This is the time when Joanne models each phase of the writing process, teaches writing skills and conventions, and provides the children with a sustained time to write. The writing block begins with a whole-class minilesson with children seated on the rug in front of a large easel. Joanne frequently begins the minilesson by rereading excerpts from the Community Reading selection or the classroom read-aloud to reinforce important text and language structures as well as vocabulary necessary for success with a writing piece. Before going off to practice a skill or strategy taught in the minilesson, students briefly share their writing plan with a peer. Three days a week, Joanne works with an English as a second language (ESL) specialist during this writing block. This arrangement allows the two teachers to provide instruction in small needs-based groups. The writing block ends with the children once again gathered on the rug to share their writing with a partner or the whole class.

Joanne has created a learning environment that engages her students in purposeful talk and in authentic reading and writing tasks that are effective for all children learning to read and write, including ELLs. She is mindful of the challenges posed by the wide range of her students' language and literacy learning needs. Joanne believes one way to respond to those needs is a nonfiction author study that can (a) increase her students' exposure to informational texts and (b) integrate reading, writing, oral language, and content instruction. To accommodate the Ann Morris author study, Joanne rearranges the sequence of reading block activities. She begins the day with small-group guided reading instruction and ends the reading block with Community

Reading. Ann Morris' books replace the anthology selections. Writing instruction follows, allowing for seamless integration of reading and writing instruction.

Ann Morris Author Study in Action

Two main factors influence our choice of author. First, the themes of Ann Morris' books, daily life and families from around the world, support Joanne's social studies curriculum. The Massachusetts History and Social Science Curriculum Framework designates second grade as the time to learn about the diversity of America's people. Children learn that there are many different customs, foods, holidays, traditions, and games throughout the world and that these differences contribute to American life. To meet this content goal, we select seven of Morris' books: *On the Go* (1990); *Houses and Homes* (1992); *Play* (1999a); *Teamwork* (1999b); *Work* (1998); *Shoes, Shoes, Shoes* (1995); and *Bread, Bread, Bread* (1989). In these texts, bright colorful photographs and a pictorial index help students explore a variety of countries and cultures throughout the world. Second graders also must be able to identify the continents and to locate their own countries of origin on a map. As previously mentioned, at the end of each book, Ann Morris provides a world map and asks the reader, "Where in the world were these photographs taken?" As the children search for the answer to this question, they apply and reinforce new knowledge about continent and country locations.

In accordance with the Curriculum Framework, students must also have opportunities to research their or their parents' or grandparents' country of origin and describe important aspects of their heritage. A second group of Ann Morris books is ideally suited to help meet this curricular goal. In the What Was It Like, Grandma? series, grandmothers from different ethnic, linguistic, and cultural groups relate family history and customs to their grandchildren. Ann Morris demonstrates how children might learn about their own families by interviewing family members, examining family artifacts such as photographs and family recipes, and constructing a family tree. We select three titles from this group, *Grandma Francisca Remembers* (2002a), *Grandma Lai Goon Remembers* (2002b), and *Grandma Lois Remembers* (2002c), because these books provide an opportunity to talk, read, and write about families that are similar to those of many of the children in Joanne's classroom.

Second, we conclude that Morris' variety of texts are ideally suited to help Joanne meet the wide range of her students' language and literacy learning needs. Books such as *On the Go*, which contains simple, consistent language structures combined with clear picture-text match, allow struggling readers and children learning English to build word knowledge and fluency as they read and reread these easy texts. The pictorial index found at the end of each of the easy texts contains additional information about the countries depicted in the books. This information is presented using sophisticated vocabulary (Weizman and Snow 2001) and more complex language structures to (a) support oral and written language development and (b) provide an appropriate challenge for average and above average readers. The What Was It Like, Grandma? series is appropriate for the able readers in Joanne's class yet is accessible as a read-aloud to those who are not reading at grade level. Taken together, these texts provide models of nonfiction text structures such as description, compare and contrast, and sequence as well the language used to organize these text structures that will guide Joanne's students as they write well-structured reports, another grade-level expectation. A curriculum map, presented in Appendix A highlights the multifaceted dimensions of this author study in conjunction with local and national standards (Massachusetts Curriculum Frameworks [ELA and social studies] and IRA/NCTE Standards for the English Language Arts).

Taking Notes On the Go

As demonstrated in the lead of this chapter, Joanna launches this nonfiction author study with an invitation for personal response to On the Go. She continues this practice throughout this author study, soliciting her second graders' personal responses to Ann Morris' nonfiction literature. Only after the children have made life-literature connects does she focus her lens on text-based instruction. For example, on the second day of the author study, Joanne begins the writing block with the children gathered on the rug in front of a large easel by returning to On the Go:

> Before I reread On the Go, I'm going to remember to ask myself a question. I wonder if the way people travel in other countries is the same as the way we travel in the United States, or is it different? First, I'm going to look back at our list of all the ways people travel in the United States. Then as I reread each page, I'm going to think about whether it is the same as the United States or whether it is different. And to help me remember important information that helps me answer that question, I will take some notes. Then, to help me organize my information, I will write my notes on a Venn diagram.

First, Joanne briefly reminds the children how notes differ from complete sentences. Together Joanne and the children decide that a good note should include a country name and a dash followed by one or two words that tell how the people in that country travel. Next, Joanne explains that she will write her information on sticky notes that she will then place on the large Venn diagram that she has placed on the easel. Joanne rereads the text and selects two pages to use to model these note-taking strategies. Joanne models using one color sticky note to indicate similarities and another color to indicate differences. Next, Joanne provides each child with a Venn diagram and asks the class to practice this note-taking process. Some children are ready to work with a partner. Joanne sends these children to work at tables on which she has placed copies of On the Go and stacks of sticky notes. Other children require much more support; therefore, Joanne and the ESL specialist work with small groups. Each group first choral reads On the Go, then takes notes, and finally organizes their notes on their Venn diagrams.

Later all the children will use their notes to form compare-and-contrast sentences, reinforcing compare-and-contrast vocabulary and sentence structures that Joanne introduced during math time. Like all of the instructional activities Joanne plans, she knows students require different levels of support to complete the task. Some children will rely on scaffolds such as patterned writing, while others will compose their own compare-and-contrast sentences.

Over the next few days, Joanne guides the children as they respond in multiple ways to several Ann Morris books during Community Reading and the writing block.

Text Analysis of Teamwork *and* Play: *How Ann Morris Organizes Her Books*

An interplay of personal and text analysis response is evident in the two titles that Joanne introduces today during community reading, *Play* and *Teamwork*. Joanne reminds the children that *On the Go* explored how people travel in other countries. She asks them to predict what Ann Morris might write about in *Play*.

"I think it is about different games from different countries," one student suggests.

"It's how people play around the world," another surmises.

As Joanne reads, hands shoot up in response to the simple text and vivid photographs. She comments, "When I see you raising your hands as I finish each page, it tells me you have something to share. It tells me you are thinking about what Ann Morris wrote, and it reminds you about something that happened to you."

Benefits of providing opportunities to respond personally accrue to both the children and Joanne. The children have additional opportunities to develop oral language skills, and Joanne learns more about her students' early experiences. Tatenda relays the following: "It makes me think about back in Africa and playing soccer and playing with my dog. He's not here. He is in Zimbabwe with my cousin. I really miss him."

Isata offers, "When I was in Africa, I didn't know how to jump rope, but when I came here I went to summer school, and they teached me. There was one jump rope song and I saw it in a book."

Joanne wonders aloud how she can find out where the photographs in *Play* were taken.

"I think Ann Morris put an index and a map in this book too," suggests Jennifer.

Together Joanne and the children select several photographs about which they would like to learn more, and Joanne reads aloud from the index. Information about making cat's cradles prompts Mariana to share that her mother knows how to do it. Isata nods her head and says "We do that in Uganda."

Joanne notices that several of the children have not shared any responses over the past two days. She reads *Teamwork* and stops to model her own personal response.

> While I was reading this book it made me think about a team that I'm a part of—my family. I'm part of that team, and we all have to work together. In the morning, we all have jobs to do. Some people have to go to work, and some people have to go to school. And when we are all working together, it's great.

Joanne's modeling encourages one child with limited English skills to share a response. Carlos reports, "I see my mom at six thirty when I get up because she come from work when I get up. She get my breakfast help me get ready for school."

Jose, a child who is often reluctant to speak in the large group adds, "My mom gives me chores, and sometimes I help in my neighborhood." Next, Joanne asks the children to turn to a partner and talk about a time that they were a member of a team. Then, she asks the children to return to their seats to first partner read *Teamwork* and then to respond to the prompt "When I read *Teamwork*, it reminds me about . . .". Samuel's response includes the many responsibilities that he has in his young life:

- doing my morning work
- making my bed
- washing my dishes
- helping my brother with he homework
- I help cleaning my mom room

From Notes to Sentences and Paragraphs

Literacy instruction in Joanne's classroom is characterized by talk about what good readers and writers do. As Joanne displays three new Ann Morris books, *Houses and Homes*; *Bread, Bread, Bread*; and *Shoes, Shoes, Shoes*, she reminds the children:

> We know that good readers ask questions before they read nonfiction books. This helps them find the information they need. But good readers also have to be certain that they choose the best book to help them learn more about a subject. If I wanted to learn more about the types of houses people live in around the world, which book would I read?

The children decide *Houses and Homes* would be the best choice. Next, Joanne introduces the term *research question*.

> To help me learn about the types of houses people live in around the world, I'm going to ask myself a research question: "What are houses in other countries like?" This helps me to find out specific information. Let's read and take some notes to help me answer my research question.

Joanne has copied her research question on a large-lined piece of paper. She reads through the text once. Again, she models using the pictorial index to learn more information about the photographs. She models note taking, writing the name of the country and the type of housing common there.

Next, Joanne turns to *Bread, Bread, Bread*. Joanne guides the children to form a good research question. They decide: "What kinds of bread do people in other countries eat?" With minimal support from Joanne, the class next provides the research question for *Shoes, Shoes, Shoes*: "What kinds of shoes do people in other countries wear?"

Joanne divides the class into three groups. She sends one group off to reread *Houses and Homes* and to take additional notes. One group works with Joanne as they choral read *Bread, Bread, Bread* and practice note-taking skills. The ESL specialist helps a third group find information in *Shoes, Shoes, Shoes*. After a read-aloud and choral reading, she guides the children to take notes on shoes around the world. Joanne meets briefly with the *Houses and Homes* group to hear what information they have learned from the pictorial index. This sequence of activities prompts Ana to ask, "I wonder why Ann Morris writes books about places all over the world?" Joanne adds another biographical question to the class' small but growing list.

Over the next several days, the writing block is devoted to teaching the children the process of turning their notes into complete sentences. Joanne takes her notes from *Houses and Homes* and demonstrates how to add details to form a complete sentence. Then Joanne turns her attention to teaching the children how to write well-formed paragraphs. Writing topic sentences requires several whole-class and small-group minilessons in which Joanne models the strategy of turning a research question into a statement for the topic sentence. Next the children work on restating their topic sentence to use as a concluding sentence. Joanne uses examples from the children's writing in each of her minilessons. Again the need to differentiate instruction is evident as some children are able to compose these sentences independently or with a partner, while others work with Joanne or the ESL specialist to form group-generated topic and concluding sentences. With differentiated levels of support, the children are engaged in researching, drafting, revising, and editing their paragraphs, filled with information from Ann Morris' books.

Also, Joanne has found time to meet with each child to identify and place a photograph on his or her country of origin. The map in Figure 3–2 underscores the children's many different language and cultural backgrounds. It is time to renew attention to personal response and to begin the preparation for a culminating writing project, a book written by each child about his or her country of origin.

What Was It Like, Grandma? *Opportunities for Multiple Response*

Grandma Francisca Remembers and *Grandma Lai Goon Remembers* provide many opportunities for the children to create oral and written personal responses. As Grandma Francisca relates family history to her granddaughter, Susanna remembers, "My grandmother told me she walked three miles to school with her brother. She lived on a farm in Puerto Rico and she had to get up early to feed the animals before school. She ate her breakfast after she fed the animals."

When Grandma Francisca teaches Angelica a family craft, Jennifer responds, "Just like Grandma Francisca taught Angelica how to make a sock doll, my grandmother taught me how to make a picture frame."

"My grandmother used to make quilts, and she gave people her quilts," adds Jason.

As the children respond to the text, many changes that the ELLs have experienced in their short lives are revealed. For example, Isata shares, "In Uganda, there was no

FIGURE 3–2 *A map showing each child's country of origin*

spring, no winter, no fall; there was just summer. And when I came here it was winter, and my stepmom had to show me how to do a lot of things and buy me clothes."

Samuel shares, "I really miss my grandmother. She doesn't live with me. She's in my country with my grandpa and my little brother."

When Joanne reads about Grandma Lai Goon, who teaches her grandchildren how to write in Chinese, Angela is inspired to name all the children in the class who know how to write Chinese. A look at Grandma Lai Goon's family tree prompts Lee, who often remains silent, to say, "My father name Pin."

Joanne smiles and responds, "That's a nice name. My father's name is Edward."

Joanne points out that in the Grandma books, Ann Morris uses many family photographs, and she writes about the people and events pictured in the family photographs. In preparation for the Grandma series, Joanne had asked each child to bring in a family photograph. The pile of photographs has grown steadily over the weeks. After reading *Grandma Lai Goon Remembers*, Joanne distributes the children's family photographs and asks each child to turn to a partner and tell a family story about the photograph he or she selected. Joanne anticipates that some of the children will not be able to produce family photographs. She has prepared a folder of magazine photographs, and she helps several children select a photograph that reminds them of a family outing or activity. Later that morning, during the writing block, the children write about their photograph. The entry in Figure 3–3, composed by Sonith, an ELL student from Cambodia, is representative of the children's responses.

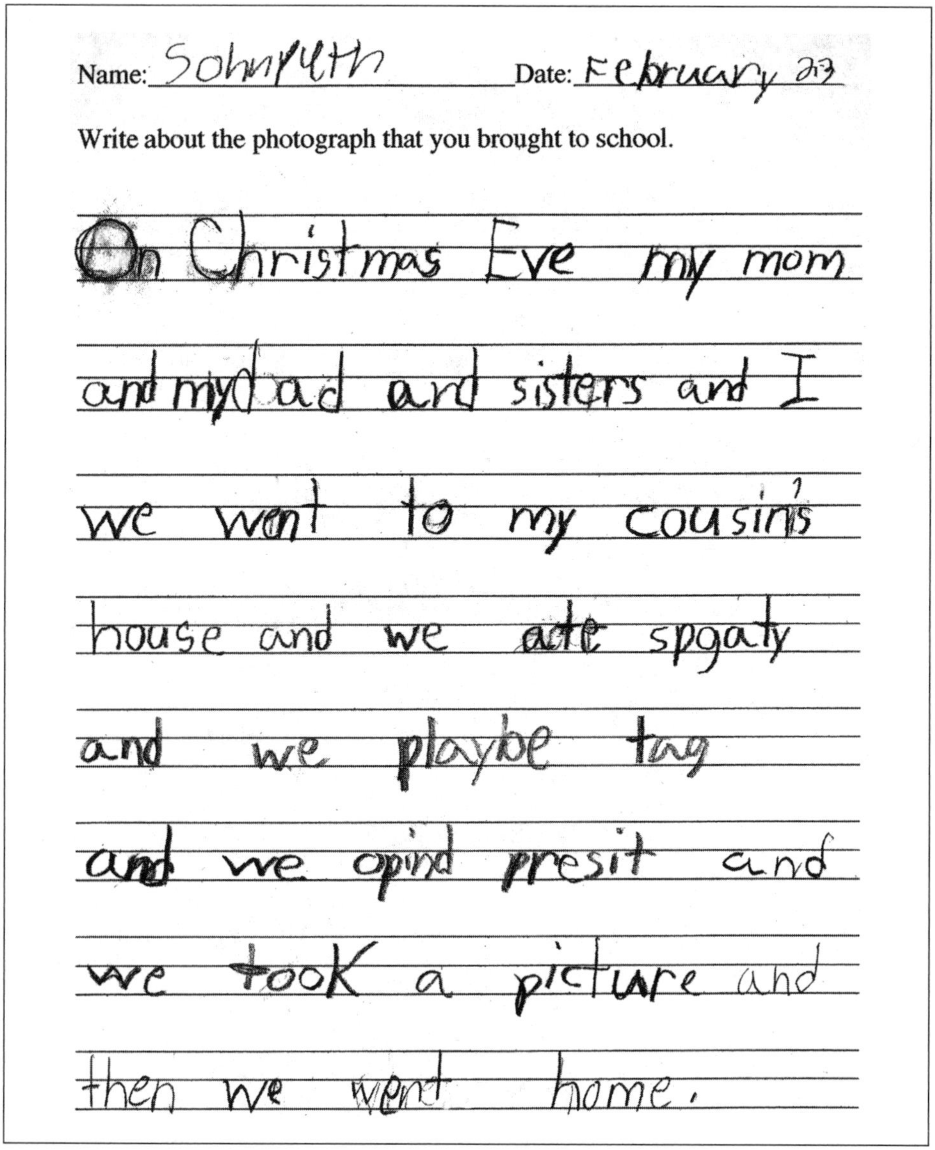

Name: Sohnruth   Date: February 23

Write about the photograph that you brought to school.

On Christmas Eve my mom
and my dad and sisters and I
we went to my cousins
house and we ate spgaty
and we playbe tag
and we opind presit and
we took a picture and
then we went home.

FIGURE 3–3   *Sonith's personal narrative*

A final Grandma book, *Grandma Lois,* is introduced. Joanne asks the children to think about what they read in *Grandma Francisca* and *Grandma Lai Goon* and to predict what they might find in this book about an African American grandmother and her family. The children quickly and confidently make their predictions.

- It will have photographs about real people.
- The grandma will tell the kids stories about their family.
- The grandma will make something with the kids.
- It has a family tree.

After a read-aloud, Joanne places a replica of her family tree on the easel and begins to talk about the members of her family. She reminds the children that her father's name is Edward, and lists her sisters and other members of her family, including her children, Patrick and Mikayla. She gives each child a copy of the blank family tree to complete at home. Over the next several days, the family trees begin to arrive in the classroom. Once Joanne has a family tree from each child, she asks the children to list all of the special things that the grandchildren in the books learned from or did with the grandmothers or other family members.

- They played checkers.
- They take walks to the market.
- They spend time together.
- She talks to the kids.

Joanne asks the children to select one member from their family tree and to write about something special they did with or learned from that person. Several of the children choose to write about family members who have remained in their home countries.

Each book in the Grandma Series provides an excellent model of the text structure of sequence. During Community Reading, Joanne points out this text structure as she focuses on the sections in which Grandma Francisca teaches Angelica how to make a traditional craft and how to prepare a family recipe. Joanne talks about why the steps must be done in a specific order, and she points out the vocabulary that is needed to introduce each step, *first, then, next, finally.* Next, Joanne asks the children to gather on the rug for the start of the writing block. This time she asks the children to bring a pencil and a clipboard, as they will work together for a brief time before going off to work independently. Joanne tells the children that when good writers want to write a how-to paper, they start with a plan that helps them organize their information. Joanne models the construction of a graphic organizer that represents the steps that Grandma Francisca took to make her favorite family recipe, again pointing out the language needed to organize each step. She then asks each child to turn to a partner and brainstorm some topics for a how-to paper and to record the ideas on a how-to handout that she distributed. Mariana's list, which is representative of the children's efforts, includes ideas such as how to make a bed, do people's hair, jump rope, clean her house, ride a bike, make a sandwich, and take a bath.

Next, Joanne sends the children back to their tables to construct a graphic organizer that represents the steps in the process they chose. James, who is from Laos, creates a graphic organizer titled "How to Make Rice," which is shown in Figure 3–4.

The following day, Joanne models how to move from the sequence graphic to a written product. For the next several days, the writing block is devoted to drafting, revising, and editing the children's how-to texts.

It is not until after the three Grandma books have been read aloud that Jennifer asks, "Do you think Ann Morris is a grandmother?" Joanne decides now is a good time to talk about Ann Morris as an author.

Who Is Ann Morris? Biographical Response

As Joanne works with two ELL students on their how-to texts, Julie asks the children to think about what they know about Ann Morris from reading her books. Their responses are largely descriptions of her books.

- She writes a lot of books. They are nonfiction books.
- She makes a map in the back of her book.
- She adds a family tree.
- She works with a photographer.
- She goes around the world.

Next, Julie asks what the children would like to know about Ann Morris. These responses reveal an interest in Ann Morris as a person. "Does she love to learn new things?" "What does she do when she is not writing?" "How is old is she?" Jennifer repeats her earlier question, "Is Ann Morris a grandmother?"

"Where will Ann Morris go next?" Angela wants to know.

Julie reads selections from the biographical information she has gathered (see Ann Morris' author profile on page 57). The children delight in learning that Ann Morris has written nearly one hundred books and that she was a teacher before she was a writer. Julie also explains that it was Morris' experience as a child in the New York public schools, surrounded by friends from many different cultural backgrounds, which sparked her lifelong interest in learning and writing about cultures other than her own. And finally, there is a gasp when Julie reads that Ann Morris is not a grandmother! Sadly, we do not find out where Ann Morris plans to travel next. Ana is not disappointed, however. "We have to keep reading her books to find out," she tells her classmates.

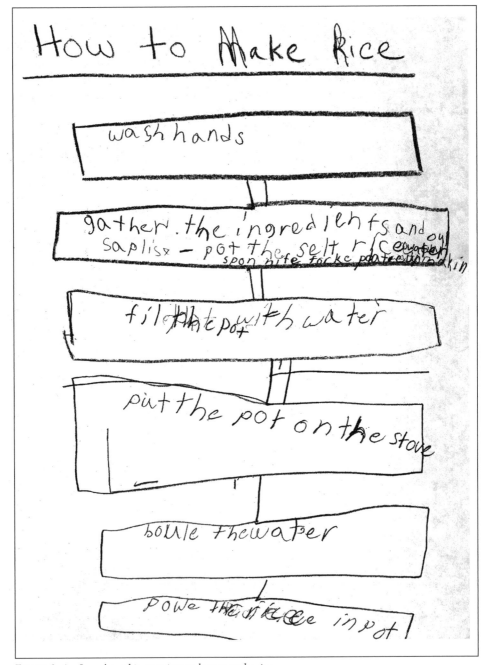

FIGURE 3–4 *James' graphic organizer on how to make rice*

Ann Morris

Born: 1921 in New York City
Careers: teacher, editor, teacher educator, author
Awards: Numerous awards including IRA-CBC Children's Choice; National Council of Social Studies Notable; NCTE Orbis Pictus Award; ALA Notable; and American Bookseller Pick of the List
Home: Manhattan, New York

Ann Morris, former classroom teacher, teacher educator, and editor is an award-winning children's book author. Although she has changed careers over the years, one interest has never changed—her love of travel. Recently, Ann has traveled to Russia to document life in a ballet school, to Israel to write about children who have experienced wars and other conflicts, and to Thailand to document the after-effects of the tsunami. This last work, *Tsunami: Helping Each Other* was named a 2005 Notable Trade Book for Young People by the National Council for Social Studies. Her fascination with and appreciation of people and places from all corners of the world are evident in her more than one hundred children's books. Ann Morris' books are filled with lush photographs; over the years she has collaborated with photographers Ken Heyman, Peter Lilenthal, and Heidi Larson. A self-described "gypsy by nature," Ann Morris (n.d.) reports, "I always have my suitcase packed." Ann Morris also travels to schools and community centers, where she helps teachers, parents, and children discover and appreciate family histories through book making workshops. When she is not traveling, Ann spends her time in Manhattan, where she loves to swim and play the piano.

Ann Morris Talks About the Grandma Series

On the inspiration for the series: "For years, I worked with Ken Heyman, who was the photographer for anthropologist Margaret Mead. From Mead, he learned that grandmothers were the ones who pass on culture" (Moms 2005, 12).

On grandmothers: "[Grandmothers] are the ones who transmit so many things to the grandchildren. They tell stories, they cook, they spend more time with the children. They collect old photographs and often they teach the family language" (Mitchell 2002, B2).

Does she wish that she were a grandmother? "You can never have it all. I'm probably around children more than many people who have children. I really enjoy my life. I've led a different kind of life and some part of me regrets some of that, and some part of me says that I would never have done half the things I've done if I'd had the other life." (Mitchell 2002, B2).

On why she wrote the series: "My hope is that the books will help kids better understand their own family history and, by recognizing the similarities that exist among all families, help them become tolerant of the differences." (Moms 2005, 12).

On preparing for the series: Peter (Lilenthal) and I went across country by car and spent almost a week with each family. I think about the book as we're moving along. For each picture in the book, Peter must take about 50 shots" (Mitchell 2002, B12)

On what she included in the series: "I tried to include things that show a grand-mother's ethnicity, culture, and religion. I also wanted to show the closeness between the grandmother and her grandchildren and all the things they do together" (Moms 2005, 12).

On her hobbies: "People watching, music in any and all forms, cat care, cooking and eating, and travel" (Morris n.d.).

Biographical References

"Ann Morris." No date. Brochure. Lothrop, Lee and Shephard.

Harper Collins. No date. "Ann Morris: Biography." Retrieved May 22, 2006 from www.harpercollins.com/global_scripts/product_catalog/author.

"An Interview with Ann Morris." 2005. *Scholastic Parent and Child*, April/May: 12.

Mitchell, E. 2002. "To Grandmothers' Houses: Author Mines Cultural Gold for Kids Series." *Newsday*, April 3, B2–B3, B12.

Morris, A. No date. Ann Morris. Retrieved May 22, 2006 from www.annmorrisbooks.com.

Ann Morris Books Used in This Author Study

Morris, A. 1989. *Bread, Bread, Bread.* New York: Lothrop, Lee and Shephard.

———. 1990. *On the Go.* New York: Lothrop, Lee and Shephard.

———. 1992. *House and Homes.* New York: Lothrop, Lee and Shephard.

———. 1995. *Shoes, Shoes, Shoes.* New York: Lothrop, Lee and Shephard.

———. 1998. *Work.* New York: Harper Collins.

———. 1999a. *Play.* New York: Lothrop, Lee and Shephard.

———. 1999b. *Teamwork.* New York: Lothrop, Lee and Shephard.

———. 2002a. *Grandma Francisca Remembers: A Hispanic-American Family Story.* What Was It Like, Grandma? Brookfield, CT: Millbrook.

———. 2002b. *Grandma Lai Goon Remembers: A Chinese-American Family Story.* What Was It Like, Grandma? Brookfield, CT: Millbrook.

———. 2002c. *Grandma Lois Remembers: An African-American Family Story.* What Was It Like, Grandma? Brookfield, CT: Millbrook.

Text Analysis: Comparing and Contrasting Ann Morris' Series Books

Joanne continues to prepare the children to write their country books. Many elements from Ann Morris' books will also be important components in the children's books. Joanne asks her second graders how the Grandma series differs from the earlier Ann Morris books that they read. The children quickly respond:

- "There's no index."
- "It doesn't have a map."
- "It has a family tree."
- "It has old family photographs."
- "It talks about how to make things."

Joanne is hopeful that as she introduces the country books to the class, elements from both series will guide the children in this project.

Writing a Country Book, Ann Morris Style

Joanne explains to the children that as part of their social studies unit, they will research and write about a country that has a special meaning for them. Joanne explains that her family is from Poland, so she will write about Poland. Joanne asks the children to take a look at the class map with their photographs (Figure 3–2) and to think about the country they might research. Nigeria, Cambodia, Brazil, Zimbabwe, and Canada are just some of the countries.

"I'm choosing Puerto Rico because my family there, and I lived there," Angela explains.

Next, Joanne asks them to think about all the Ann Morris books that they have read and to help her generate a list of items that should be included in their country books. This list grows quickly. A map, an index, a table of contents, a family tree, favorite foods, recipes, and games are just some of the suggestions. Joanne is pleased to discover that the children have spontaneously listed elements from the two Ann Morris series they have studied. Next, Joanne and the children brainstorm where they will find the information they will need to write the country books. Among the first responses Joanne records are books, the Internet, and encyclopedias, but soon Joanne is able to record a true Ann Morris response, "I can ask my grandma!"

The next day, during Community Reading, Joanne reads aloud from her own country book. Joanne's book will remain the model for each child's book. At the tables, Joanne has placed copies of books about the various countries for children to browse through during independent reading time. The actual writing of the children's individual country books extended far beyond the author study. Finding nonfiction books on each country at the children's independent reading levels was challenging. For several children, Joanne was unable to provide a book, and these children had to rely on information from the Internet that some were able to read independently. For others, Joanne had to rewrite to simplify the information. Weeks of forming research questions, reading, and note taking followed. As in each phase of the author study, children continued to need different levels of support to complete their research. Some children relied on written scaffolds to form their questions (e.g., What are some of the typical foods in _____ [country]?). Others were able to form research questions independently, as seen in Figure 3–5.

Writing and publishing each page of the country book required minilessons on forming topic sentences, turning notes into complete sentences, and writing concluding sentences. Figure 3–6 presents Tatenda's eleven-page Zimbabwe book, minus the cover page, map of Zimbabwe, and family tree.

The art teacher offered to help the children make papier-mâché globes that they painted and labeled highlighting their country of origin. Joanne hosted a family coffee at which the children displayed their globes and books. A class trip to a cultural festival that featured music and folk dances from around the world was a fitting celebration of the children's look around the world that began with *On the Go!*

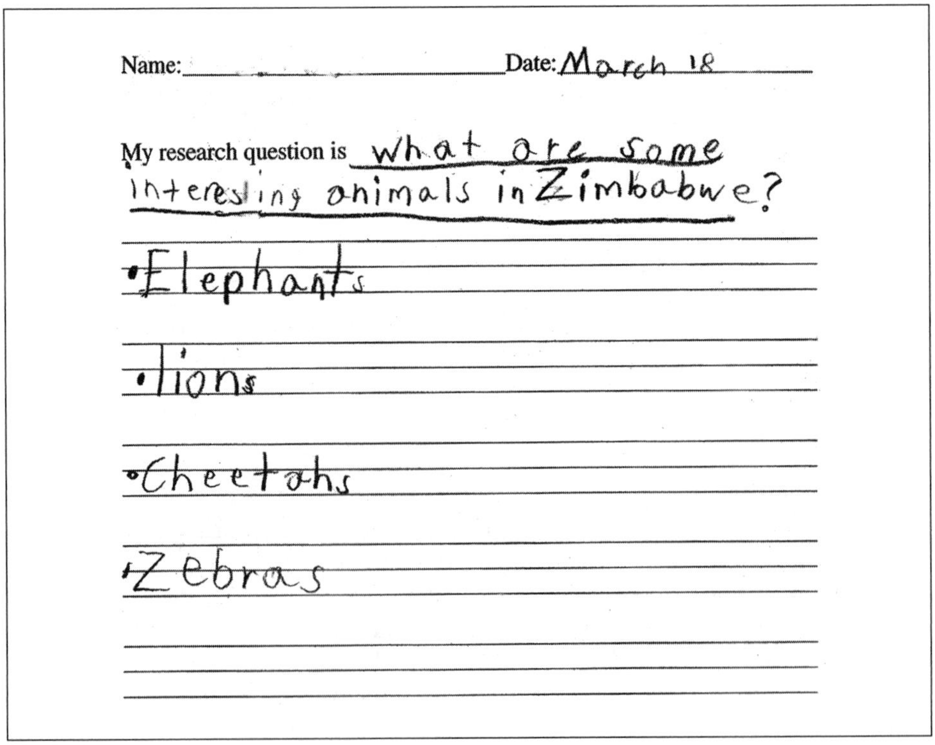

Name: _____ Date: March 18 _____

My research question is What are some interesting animals in Zimbabwe?

• Elephants

• lions

• Cheetahs

• Zebras

FIGURE 3–5   *Tatenda's research question*

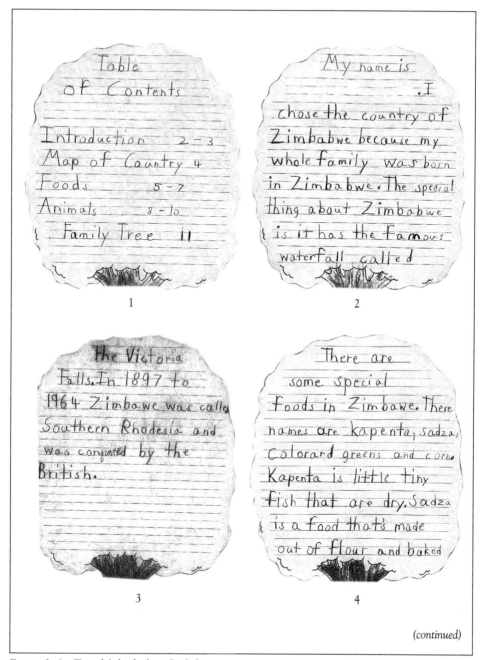

1

Table
of Contents

2

My name is
_____ . I
chose the country of
Zimbabwe because my
whole family was born
in Zimbabwe. The special
thing about Zimbabwe
is it has the famous
waterfall called

3

the Victoria
Falls. In 1897 to
1964 Zimbawe was called
Southern Rhodesia and
was conquered by the
British.

4

There are
some special
foods in Zimbawe. There
names are kapenta, sadza,
colorard greens and corn.
Kapenta is little tiny
fish that are dry. Sadza
is a food that's made
out of flour and baked

(continued)

FIGURE 3–6   *Tatenda's book about Zimbabwe*

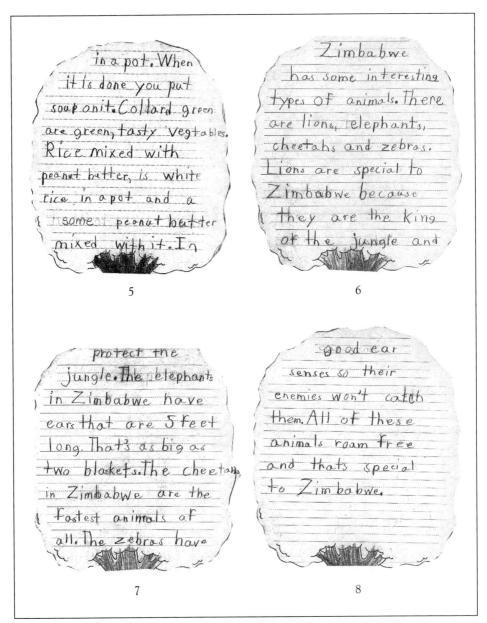

5

in a pot. When
it is done you put
soup on it. Collard green
are green, tasty vegtables.
Rice mixed with
peanut butter, is white
rice in a pot and a
some peanut butter
mixed with it. In

6

Zimbabwe
has some interesting
types of animals. There
are lions, elephants,
cheetahs and zebras.
Lions are special to
Zimbabwe because
they are the king
of the jungle and

7

protect the
jungle. The elephants
in Zimbabwe have
ears that are 5 feet
long. That's as big as
two blankets. The cheetahs
in Zimbabwe are the
fastest animals of
all. The zebras have

8

good ear
senses so their
enemies won't catch
them. All of these
animals roam free
and thats special
to Zimbabwe.

FIGURE 3–6   (Continued)

Concluding Comments

The children's interests and unflagging desire for more and more Ann Morris books kept the focus on Ann Morris much longer than we anticipated. We enlisted the help of the school librarian, who found *Karate Boy* (1996), *Weddings* (1995), *Loving* (1990), *Tools* (1992), and the remainder of the series What Was It Like, Grandma? (2002–2003). Joanne located several titles from the series That's Our School! (2003)—a new Ann Morris series that we did not include in our author study. Each book was added to the growing display of Ann Morris books that children returned to over and over during independent reading time. When asked to name a favorite Ann Morris book, many of the children listed books that were not the focus of the author study but that Joanne had made available. The school librarian, the ESL specialist, the art teacher, and the children's parents and guardians were integral components of this successful project. The parent-teacher association donated funds for the field trip and a statewide literacy organization donated funds to purchase copies of many of the Ann Morris books.

An invaluable aspect of the Ann Morris author study was that it provided meaningful and authentic opportunities for ELLs to develop oral and written language skills as they were learning grade-level content. During Community Reading, children listened to or read an Ann Morris book and then had opportunities to respond personally both orally and in writing. Joanne routinely pointed out important nonfiction text structures, language used to organize the texts, and nonfiction text features that children might use as they were writing each day during the writing block and later as they wrote their country books. Independent reading time provided another opportunity to read and respond to an Ann Morris book. Joanne's consistent attention to modeling and providing opportunities for guided and independent practice of skills promoted use of academic vocabulary as well as repeated opportunities for purposeful reading, writing, and talking. In addition to eliciting personal and text-based responses, Joanna also brought the woman behind these cherished books to life. Ann Morris had become a friend and a mentor.

Meeting ELLs' language and literacy learning needs is a challenge that more and more classroom teachers are facing. We hope that our experiences will encourage other teachers who are just beginning to work with ELLs and those who are experienced to venture into the study of nonfiction authors as they strive to help their students gain the language and literacy skills and content knowledge necessary for school success.

4

All About Arnosky
Grade 3

Patricia Harris

On the first day of our author study, my third graders arrive to find a copy of a photograph with the following caption taped to their desks: "Hello, my name is Jim Arnosky. Can you guess my occupation?" After entertaining a few possibilities, I explain: "When we read stories, we read between the lines to make inferences. Today we will be working as detectives to make inferences in a different way. We will be looking at clues that will help us figure out who Jim Arnosky is."

I then direct the students' attention to a small suitcase at the front of the room. I ask the class to pretend that this suitcase belongs to Arnosky and that he has given us permission to look inside. I explain that we will be unpacking his suitcase (Laney and Mosely 1990) and analyzing its contents in order to solve our mystery. My third graders are intrigued.

Prior to the students' arrival, I packed the suitcase with items that related to Jim Arnosky. For example, because Arnosky illustrates his own books, I packed some tubes of acrylic paint and several paintbrushes. Figure 4–1 shows the items that the students would find in each layer of the suitcase. The items were layered from general to specific so that as the students delved deeper into the suitcase, they could refine their inferences (Laney and Mosely 1990).

One student helps me unpack, showing and describing each item from the first layer, as I solicit biographical connections from the class. For example, when we unpack the map of Vermont, Melissa suggests that perhaps Arnosky lives in Vermont. Thomas thinks it tells us where he was born. I then pass out a template and ask that the children keep track of their inferences as we move through the layers in the suitcase. Figure 4–2 presents Thomas' completed template. For the third layer (containing a notebook and pencil), Brendan suggests that Arnosky writes stories. Edmund thinks he might be a reporter. Kylie thinks he uses the tools to draw pictures. Again we record our inferences. As the last layer of the suitcase—Arnosky's books—is unpacked, Megan infers that Arnosky writes books. When I ask for evidence, Megan is quick to identify Arnosky's name on the covers. The mystery is solved. I then confirm that Arnosky is

FIGURE 4–1   *Items in Jim Arnosky's suitcase*

an author-illustrator of many awarding-winning books who lives in Vermont. I note that I am a fan of Arnosky's work and am excited that we will be learning more about him and his books over the next few weeks.

My Classroom

My students—twelve girls and twelve boys—attend a public elementary school in a middle-class town. While some of my students are reading above grade-level and capable of completing grade level work independently, some are reading significantly below grade-level and require modified instruction and support to complete grade level assignments. Naturally, many students fall between these two academic extremes. My special education population includes students with disabilities ranging from specific learning disabilities to communication disabilities. In addition, four of these children have been diagnosed with attention deficit. Because seven receive special education services, I have two full-time instructional aides helping me implement their individualized education plans.

Given this range of abilities, I choose Arnosky because I am confident that his books will not only intrigue my students but also support their entrée to nonfiction

Who Packed the Suitcase?

Name: *Thomas*   Date: _____

Layer 1

Object	What does it tell you about the person?
name tag	His name is Jim Arnosky
date September 1, 1946	his birthday?
map of Vermont	going there? lives there? born there?

Who might the person be? *farmer*

Layer 2

Object	What does it tell you about the person?
paint	he paints
paint brushes	he's an artist

Who might the person be? *painter*

Who Packed the Suitcase?

Name: *Thomas*   Date: _____

Layer 3

Object	What does it tell you about the person?
video tape "Backyard Safari"	director? animator? TV show?
notebook and pencil	writes stories? reporter? sketchbook?

Who might the person be? *draws pictures for tv show*

Layer 4

Object	What does it tell you about the person?
web address	has his own website works on a computer
award	award winning work
books	he writes books

Who might the person be? *an author*

Who is this person? *an author*

FIGURE 4–2   *Thomas' template*

literature. As a naturalist, Arnosky has a gift for observing, drawing, and writing about the world around him. His All About books contain detailed, accurate illustrations of animals as well as sparse but engaging text that fosters inquiry. Because Arnosky's work has the potential to awaken a love of nonfiction for struggling readers (Caswell and Duke 1998) and because it dovetails perfectly with my science curriculum, I invite him to mentor my young writers.

The literacy program in my school is anchored in an anthology from a well-known publisher. This anthology is divided into themes. Each theme contains three to four full-length, grade-appropriate selections in addition to poems, brief nonfiction texts, comics, and other short reading selections that tie to the theme. The publisher outlines specific skills to be taught with each story including but not limited to comprehension, grammar, writing, and vocabulary. These skills have been carefully selected to address the *Massachusetts English Language Arts Curriculum Framework*. I supplement the anthology with picture storybooks, nonfiction literature, and chapter books. My students engage in independent reading, literature circles, and shared reading, both as a whole class and in small groups. I also read aloud to my students every day.

I meet the challenge of weaving an author study into an already tight curriculum by substituting Arnosky's books for the nonfiction selections in the anthology. I use Arnosky's books to teach the skills outlined in the anthology in accordance with the *Framework*. Specifically, my students learn about nonfiction text features, distinguish fact from fiction, identify main ideas and supporting details, and implement basic research by generating questions, gathering information from several sources, and writing reports.

Arnosky Author Study in Action

I implement this author study (originally coplanned with my colleague, Heather Johnson) across a four-week span during the month of May. Having launched the author study with the suitcase activity discussed in the opening of this chapter, I then flood my classroom with Arnosky's books. Because none of my students have experienced an author study of any kind in previous years, I want to instill an appreciation for what it is that nonfiction writers do as they devote themselves to the study of topics that intrigue them, and in the process inspire young writers to do the same. In addition, with each Arnosky book read, I solicit both personal response and prior knowledge to acknowledge students' life experiences and ways of knowing. Analysis of Arnosky's texts follows as my young writers examine how he organizes and presents his content and integrates visual displays. My students then try their hand at composing nonfiction text.

The sequence of curricular events and corresponding local and national standards (Massachusetts Curriculum Frameworks [ELA and science] and IRA/NCTE Standards for the English Language Arts) are presented in a curriculum map in Appendix A.

Browsing Arnosky's Books

Because I think it is important for students to see the breadth and depth of Arnosky's work, I gather thirty of his books from my own collection and the public library. I place a stack of books at each table and ask students to select and browse through one book. After a minute, I ask the students to return that book to the stack and select another. We continue this way until each student has looked at every book in the stack. Then I rotate the stacks of books from group to group and repeat the process two more times. They are amazed at the number of books that Arnosky has written. I then assign a writing prompt to see what observations the students have made about Arnosky's books. Like Robert (see Figure 4–3), many conclude that Arnosky writes mostly about animals and other nature topics as well as informational storybooks, like the Crinkleroot series, which merge fiction and nonfiction. A few animal-based fictional picture books such as *The Rattlesnake Dance* (2000b) and *Rabbits and Raindrops* (1997) are also in the mix.

During the discussion, Sara wonders if Arnosky or his father is Crinkleroot, the jolly woodsman who resembles Santa Claus in the Crinkleroot series. I ask what prompts this connection. She replies that Crinkleroot reminds her of the photograph of Arnosky. I ask the students to take out their photos of Arnosky and compare them to Crinkleroot's illustration. Many concur with Sara's hunch. I move to the chart pack and record her speculation, explaining that as we move through the author study, we'll try to find out more about Crinkleroot and Arnosky. I encourage others to add their hunches to our chart. Biographical response has begun.

Identifying Text Features in Nonfiction Literature

Today's lesson begins with the class's earlier observation that Arnosky writes both nonfiction and fiction. I ask about the difference between these genres. Sean states, "Fiction is a made-up story. Nonfiction is facts." I inform the class that because the bulk of Arnosky's work is nonfiction, we need to have a good understanding of what nonfiction is. With an assortment of nonfiction trade books in hand such as *Rocks and Minerals* (Symes 1988), *A Drop of Water* (Wick 1997), and *Leonardo Da Vinci* (Stanley 1997), I ask the class to form a reading train, a grouping arrangement that we have used many times. Students arrange their chairs in a straight line, one student behind the other. I distribute one book to each student. After a minute or two of browsing, I ask the students to pass their book to the person in front of them. The student at the front of the line walks her book to the student at the end of the line. They spend fifteen minutes passing and browsing books in the same manner.

The students then return to their desks with the last book that they had an opportunity to browse. I comment, "Recall our field trip to the public library when the children's librarian introduced us to the features of nonfiction books." To tap into this prior knowledge, I show them the nonfiction book that I was browsing. "This book has a table of contents. How many of you noticed a table of contents in one of the books

Name: _Robert_   Number: _14_

As you browsed through Jim Arnosky's many books, you may have noticed some common themes, features, or topics. What did you discover about the types of books that Jim Arnosky writes?

The books that Jim Arnosky writes are based on a lot of nature and animals, too. He writes books mostly all facts. Or you could call it nonfiction. Also he writes Crinkleroot books. The stories are mostly based outdoors. Some of his books start with ALL ABout then there's ALL ABout Turkeys, Turtles, owls, rattlesnakes. Also books like He has some How To Do books. He writes Same types of info but about different animals

FIGURE 4–3   *Robert's observations about Arnosky's books*

you were skimming?" Many hands go up. I write *table of contents* on the board and ask, "How does a table of contents help a reader?"

Nichole responds, "It tells you where the chapters start."

I concur that that is one piece of information in a table of contents and ask the students to check for a table of contents in their book and to think about other information conveyed. The students confirm that the majority of the books contain a table of contents and add that a table of contents tells all the major topics addressed in a book. I continue, "What other text features do authors use to help readers locate and make sense of the information in books?"

Matthew notes, "My book has an index in the back."

"What's an index?" I ask.

He replies, "It tells you what page to look on for all different things."

The students check their books for indexes and confirm that most contain this feature. We add the word *index* under *table of contents*. The students continue raising their hands to offer ideas. As each idea is presented, the other students search their books for the feature in question. They eventually generate the following list of features on the front board: table of contents, index, glossary, section headings, maps, diagrams, photographs, illustrations, captions, and important words in bold print. I announce that in our next lesson we will examine Jim Arnosky's nonfiction books to discover which of these features occur in his books.

Analyzing Text Features in Arnosky's Books

I hand out a checklist containing the nonfiction features generated in the previous session. Students then choose four books from a stack of Arnosky's books and complete this checklist for each (see Figure 4–4). A number of interesting findings are shared. Brett notes, "I didn't have a lot of checks."

Danielle agrees, "He doesn't use a lot of these things in his books."

I ask, "What does he use?"

Brian offers, "Illustrations and captions." I ask each student to find an example of an illustration and caption in an Arnosky book and point to it. I walk around the classroom, checking responses and asking a few children to explain the relationship between an illustration and a caption. They note that some captions identify a species while others give specific, interesting details about a species. Brian comments that Arnosky is a really good artist and wonders if he draws things other than animals and their habitats. I compliment his speculation about Arnosky, add it to our hunch chart, and note that we will have a chance to talk more about Arnosky, the person and the writer, in an upcoming lesson. Then I redirect their attention to the task at hand and ask if anyone found any other features.

Joe suggests, "Diagrams." Again, I ask my students to find a diagram and monitor for understanding.

I inquire, "Anything else?"

Kylie says, "I found a table of contents in one book."

Name: _Kylie_ Number: _15_

Text Organization in Jim Arnosky's Books

Directions: Look at four different Jim Arnosky books. For each one you look at record the title below. Then check off the features that the book has.

Title: _Crinderoots guide to knowing Butterfly's and Moths_

Table of Contents	____	Photographs	
Glossary	____	Illustrations	✓
Index	____	Maps	✓
Topic Headings	____	Diagrams	✓
Key Words in Bold Print	____	Captions	✓

Title: _Fish in a Flash_

Table of Contents	✓	Photographs	✓
Glossary	____	Illustrations	✓
Index	✗	Maps	____
Topic Headings	✗	Diagrams	✗
Key Words in Bold Print	✗	Captions	✓

Title: _Books of Animals Tracks and Wildlife Signs_

Table of Contents	____	Photographs	
Glossary	____	Illustrations	✓
Index	✗	Maps	____
Topic Headings	✓	Diagrams	____
Key Words in Bold Print	____	Captions	✓

Title: _All about Alligators_

Table of Contents	____	Photographs	
Glossary	____	Illustrations	✓
Index	____	Maps	✓
Topic Headings	✗	Diagrams	✓
Key Words in Bold Print	____	Captions	✓

FIGURE 4–4   *Kylie's checklist of nonfiction text features*

I survey the class, "Did anyone else find a table of contents?" Only a few hands go up. As the discussion continues, we decide that Jim Arnosky does not use many of the text features that we noted in other nonfiction books. Most of his books do not include a table of contents, a glossary, an index, topic or section headings, photographs, or important words in boldface. I ask why they think Arnosky chose not to include these access features. We talk about the limited amount of print in the All About books, compared with some of the books we examined in the previous session. I show other comparable books, such as Maestro's *A Sea Full of Sharks* (1990) and Cole's *Hungry, Hungry Sharks* (1986). I explain that when authors are writing for younger readers, they work hard to include only the most important information in their books so that readers aren't overwhelmed. Because each page often contains only a paragraph, they don't divide the content in headings and so forth. Instead, some authors like Arnosky rely heavily on the use of illustrations, maps, diagrams, and captions. I end this lesson by encouraging the students to pay careful attention to these features as they read his books.

All About Frogs: *Personal Response and Prior Knowledge*

Because Arnosky's All About books garnered the most interest during the earlier browsing session, I decide to anchor instruction on headings, main ideas, and details in his *All About Frogs* (2002a) over the next few lessons. To begin today's lesson, I introduce this book and ask if anyone has ever seen a frog. Hands fly; the children are eager to relate their frog encounters. After fielding two responses, I announce that I am eager to learn about their experiences with frogs. I pass out the writing prompt; everyone is primed to write. Like Brian (see Figure 4–5), many write about a time they or a friend or family member caught a frog. In general, students write about where they found the frog, what it looked like, and what they did with the frog when they found it. One student writes about how it made him feel when he returned a frog to its natural environment. This opportunity for personal response generates a high level of excitement and engagement.

Capitalizing on the prior knowledge contained in some of their personal responses, I challenge them to show just how much they know about frogs before we even read Arnosky's book. I pass out an anticipation guide (see examples of anticipation guides in Chapter 6) that contains ten statements about frogs and explain that they must decide whether each statement is true or false. Because this is the first time they have used an anticipation guide, we complete the first two items together. Students then complete the rest of the guide on their own.

During the next session, we review our responses to the anticipation guide, tallying yes and no votes. I explain that we'll find out which statements are accurate as we read *All About Frogs*. Each child is given a copy of the book and assigned to a reading group. One group follows along in the book as a classroom aide reads the text; she stops at appropriate places to pose questions, clarify meaning, and check for understanding. Another group meets with me, each taking turns reading the text aloud and monitoring

Brian

**Write about a time when you or someone you
know encountered a frog. What happened and
how did it make you feel?**

Two of my cousins
once were playing
in the woods in
the back of their houses, when
they caught a frog smaller
than a quarter. One kept it
for a few days. My brother saw
it and told me how cool it
was. He said it's color was cool,
orange with black spots. I went
to see it one day, but my cousin
had set it free five minutes before.
I was dissapointed that I didn't
get to see my cousins frog.

FIGURE 4–5 *Brian's personal response to* All About Frogs

for comprehension. The remaining students stay at their seats and read the book independently using a whisper voice as my other classroom aide circulates. He pulls up a chair next to each student and listens to him or her read for a bit, providing assistance if needed.

After the groups have finished reading, we return to the anticipation guides. The students use a crayon to correct their guide. For statements about which students are uncertain, we return to the book to verify the facts. Thus, the anticipation guide has served two purposes. As a prereading activity, it has stimulated the students' prior knowledge of frogs. As a postreading activity, it has served as a comprehension check and provided an opportunity to skim the text to verify facts.

Generating Headings for All About Frogs

I post the chart created in an earlier session that lists the features of nonfiction books. I ask the class to recall what we meant when we said that most nonfiction books contain headings. Brian offers, "It's the part that tells what it's going to be about." I concur and move on to the next activity, explained in the next paragraph. In hindsight, I realize I should have developed the concept of heading more fully. Next time I implement this author study, for example, I plan to place the section containing the heading "Saltopus" in Simon's *The Smallest Dinosaurs* (1982) on the overhead and ask what we should expect to find in this section. After fielding answers, I will ask if we will also learn about T-rex in this section on the *Saltopus*. I will read a few more headings in *The Smallest Dinosaurs* and ask them to conclude how Simon has organized this book (e.g., by dinosaur). I will explain that a heading is a title or main idea that summarizes what the passage is about. I will then introduce Simon's *New Questions and Answers About Dinosaurs* (1990), read the heading "What Color Were the Dinosaurs?" and ask what kind of content a reader should expect. After a few more examples from this book, I will ask how the headings of these two books differ and why. Hopefully, they will conclude that writers first decide what information they want to present and then figure out the best way to organize this information, using headings when appropriate.

Returning to the lesson, I remind the children that when we looked at many of Arnosky's books, we didn't find headings. I note how helpful headings are to readers and wonder whether we could generate headings for Arnosky's passages. They are confident that they can. I place the opening page of *All About Frogs* on the overhead:

> Frogs, toads, and salamanders are amphibians. Amphibians are animals that begin life in the water as tadpoles. They slowly develop limbs and lungs and eventually live primarily on land.
>
> All amphibians are cold-blooded. They warm up in the sun and cool off in the shade. Frogs hop into the water to cool off and to keep safe from hungry predators. (unnumbered)

I record two headings on the board: "The Enemies of Amphibians" and "What Are Amphibians?" I ask which heading fits the passage we just read. They are quick to select the latter and explain why. I retort, though, that the passage mentions predators and ask why they didn't choose the first heading. They defend their decision with ease. We repeat this process with another passage from the book. I reiterate that headings help writers organize their information and readers find information quickly. I add that it would be great if they would generate headings for *All About Frogs* so that future readers could more easily access information of interest.

Partners are assigned one page in *All About Frogs*. Arnosky's All About books lend themselves well to this task because generally each page covers one topic, such as body parts, life cycle, or eating habits. Student pairs read the assigned page and discuss ideas for a heading. The classroom aides and I monitor, offering assistance. After a pair drafts its heading on scrap paper and confers with one of us, the two record the heading on an index card. Over the next two days, each pair reads its page to the class and presents the heading. We tape the index card onto that page in the book for permanent reference.

After reviewing the key categories of information noted in *All About Frogs*, I ask whether they think Arnosky uses many of the same categories for his other All About books. They are quite certain that he does. I suggest that we investigate these books to confirm our hypothesis. I ask each child to sign up to read one of Arnosky's All About books. The students can choose *All About Alligators* (1994), *All About Deer* (1996a), *All About Owls* (1999a), *All About Rattlesnakes* (2002b), or *All About Turtles* (2000a). I pass out the books and explain that as they read their book, they should record a heading for each section on a sticky note. Because each page (or two-page spread) essentially introduces a separate category of content, this works well. Most accomplish this task accurately and independently; some need support. Overall, I am impressed with their efforts. In particular, I am struck by their high level of investment in generating headings for each section of their Arnosky book. Initial instruction in main ideas and details had occurred earlier in the year; students designed main idea statements for passages. Although they are essentially doing the same task during the author study, they now bring energy and insight to the task because they have a purpose for generating these headings—to enhance Arnosky's work and to help future readers.

Analyzing Topic Sentences in Arnosky's Paragraphs

Having discussed how Arnosky organizes his information across a book, I shift our focus to how he organizes information at the paragraph level. We begin with a review of the concept of a stated main idea. I present each sentence of the following paragraph from *All About Frogs* on a strip of a transparency:

> Only male frogs make sounds. They call to attract female frogs. Frogs produce sounds by inflating vocal sacs in their throats and vibrating the air as they slowly let it out. Some species inflate one large vocal sac. Others inflate two small vocal sacs. The sound each species of frog makes when calling is as distinctive as the species color and markings. (2002a, unnumbered)

I then draw my hand on the bottom of the transparency and ask which sentence contains the main idea or topic sentence of the passage. Because they have had instruction in main ideas, they tell me to place the first sentence on the palm of the hand. I ask why they think this is the topic sentence. I confirm that the first sentence usually, but not always, contains the main idea. I note that if this is the main idea, all the remaining details must support it. As I place each detail on a finger, I ask for justification. My third graders explain the main idea–detail relationship. I reinforce the idea that just as the palm of the hand holds all of the fingers together, so too the main idea sentence holds all of the details of a paragraph together.

I then present sentences from a passage from *All About Sharks* (2003), which we have not read during our author study, on the fingers:

> Never go in the ocean with an unhealed cut.
>
> Wade only where you can see the ocean floor; avoid murky water.
>
> Never go swimming in the ocean at night.
>
> Never touch a small or injured shark; it can still bite you. (unnumbered)

This time, they must craft the main idea. I record various versions (e.g., "Here are some rules to avoid shark attacks," "Sharks are very dangerous," and "Sharks are dangerous so follow these rules to avoid them!") on the palm. We discuss the relationship of each suggestion to the details and choose the one that best represents the main idea. I reveal Arnosky's heading, "Shark Safety Tips" (which I turn into a main idea); they are quite pleased that they were able to approximate it. I then pass out a hands worksheet and direct them to read the details on the fingers and write a main idea on the "palm" for three subsequent passages from *All About Sharks*.

"Five Frog Facts" Pamphlet: Learning to Paraphrase

To this point, we have discussed how nonfiction authors organize their content in terms of headings and topic sentences. To ready the students for a research project, which is described in the next section, I have one more important concept to address: paraphrasing. I introduce this difficult concept by showing them the pamphlet cover that I have made, titled "Five Frog Facts."

I explain that I reread *All About Frogs* and chose what I thought were five important facts. I record the following sentence from *All About Frogs* on the board: "Frogs and toads are similar but different animals" (2002a, unnumbered). I ask if I can just copy this sentence that Arnosky wrote on my pamphlet. Thomas replies, "We shouldn't just copy it because that's like stealing."

I tell the class that Tom is right: "Copying this sentence word for word or even just a few words from this book or any material would be stealing. We would be stealing Arnosky's words and taking credit for them. That's not fair to Jim Arnosky, is it? So instead, we must write his ideas in our own words and give him credit. We call this paraphrasing. Today we are all going to practice paraphrasing facts from *All About Frogs* so that we can complete our pamphlets."

I then do a think-aloud. I reread Arnosky's original and say: "OK, what is the big idea that I have learned? Frogs and toads may look the same, but they are not the same animal. Let me try to write a paraphrase of Arnosky's sentence: *Frogs and toads are not the same animal even though they look alike.*" I ask the class how else I might express the same ideas. I record "Frogs look a lot like toads" and ask them to help me finish the sentence. They offer "but they aren't the same." I note that both the sentences convey the same message that Arnosky wrote, but that they are written in our own words. I also emphasize that we need to acknowledge that we got our information from Arnosky, citing him at the end of our pamphlet.

We continue to practice paraphrasing other sentences from other All About books. When they demonstrate a basic understanding, I hand out a piece of green construction paper, which they fold in half. On the front, they write "Five Frog Facts" and their name. Edmund adds the words *ribbit, ribbit* to the cover of his pamphlet. I tell them that they may add some illustrations. Kaitlin chooses to draw three green lily pads. Melissa opts to draw a frog head with large bulging eyes and a speech bubble coming from his mouth that says, "by Melissa." They then begin independently paraphrasing the facts from the frog book. Students who are still struggling with the concept move to the back table to receive further instruction. Figure 4–6 presents Matthew's five paraphrased frog facts.

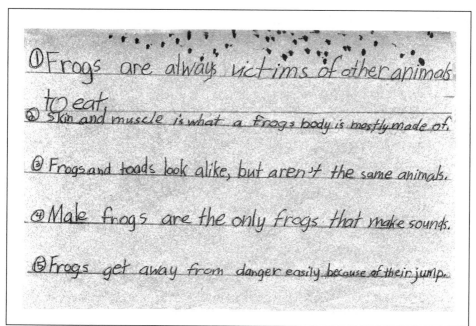

FIGURE 4–6 *Matthew's paraphrased facts about frogs*

I Have a Hunch About Arnosky!

Other than the information learned during the Unpack the Suitcase activity or read on the author's book jackets, the students have been given no biographical information up to this point. I post the hunch chart and review ideas generated to this point. To encourage further speculations, I say, "Now that we've had a chance to read some of Jim Arnosky's books, I'm wondering if you can make other guesses about him as a person and a writer."

In keeping with Arnosky's nature theme, I pass out leaf-shaped sticky notes and ask my students to write their hunches. Each then reads his or her entry, placing it on the three-foot hunch tree that Brian and Sean drew earlier in the week and posted on a bulletin board. Their speculations traverse the personal and the professional:

- I think he loves animals and will do anything to protect them.
- I think Arnosky travels all over the world to find out what animals do.
- He likes nature, hunting and he lives in a mobile home.
- I think ever since Jim Arnosky was little he was interested in nature.
- He probably lives in the country and I think he doesn't live in the city. He has a lot of experience for nature.

We surmise that Arnosky is a nature lover who uses his words and illustrations to make others want to care for animals and that this love of animals probably began when he was a youngster. I explain that in a subsequent lesson we will learn which of our hunches are correct.

Creating an Animal Ark: Arnosky Mentors Our Report Writing

Arnosky's Ark (1999b) provides the impetus for our first research report. I begin by writing the words *extinct* and *endangered* on the board and asking if anyone knows their meaning. Robert says, "*Extinct* means gone forever, like the dinosaurs are." I confirm that *extinct* is used to talk about a species, or kind of animal, that no longer exists.

"What about *endangered?*" I ask.

Joe answers, "It's like an animal that is almost extinct but not yet."

"So when we use the term *endangered species,*" I say, "we are referring to a species that is in danger of becoming extinct." I show *Arnosky's Ark* and explain it is a book Arnosky wrote about animals that were once endangered but, because humans helped them to survive, are no longer in jeopardy.

Because this book is long, I choose to read aloud over two days the introduction and the entries on the alligator, the cougar, the black bear, the manatee, and the gorilla as well as the last page of the book, in which Arnosky invites his readers to create their own ark of endangered species. I ask what they think about his idea. They are hooked. I tell them that I did some preliminary research to identify endangered species not mentioned by Arnosky. I post a list of species, organized under the following categories: mammals, birds, fish, reptiles, and amphibians. Students sign up for a category and then select one species. I explain that as they research their animal, they will put into practice what we have learned about paraphrasing content and paragraph writing. Each will write a paragraph about an endangered species and place it in our ark.

My aides and I fill the room with resource materials containing information from the classroom and school libraries and the Internet, tagged with sticky notes to facilitate easy access. With our help, each student locates appropriate material.

To figure out what our paragraphs might include, we analyze Arnosky's entry on the osprey. The lead paragraph reads:

> Of all the birds of prey, ospreys are my favorite. I love the way they fly high over the water and suddenly dive, plunging to catch a fish. For my ark, I chose a family of osprey that had built their great nest high atop a platform. (1999b, unnumbered)

We decide that Arnosky begins his entry with facts that he loves about the osprey. We then note that he tells why the osprey became endangered in the next paragraph. We agree that this is a good model for our reports. Using a note-taking worksheet mirroring Arnosky's model, my students read and record their information with reminders about (and reteaching in some cases) paraphrasing information and attribution. Discussions about selecting important facts and key reasons for endangerment are ongoing.

Each writes a rough draft and then confers with us for feedback. After the piece has been revised and edited, they write a final copy and draw an illustration of their endangered species. At their suggestion, we then assemble their paragraphs and illustrations into a class book called *Animal Ark*. Figure 4–7 shows Michael's contribution to *Animal Ark*.

Ready to put finishing touches on our class book, I remind them that Arnosky included a dedication and an introduction in his *Ark* book. We decide that our book should do the same. On a piece of chart paper, we brainstorm a list of people to whom we could dedicate our book. After some discussion, we decide to dedicate it to Jim Arnosky for inspiring us to write the book and to the endangered wildlife about which we have learned. We then brainstorm ideas for the introduction of our book. I serve as the recorder, jotting down ideas and guiding revisions. Our introduction reads:

> We decided to make our own ark because we learned that there are a lot of endangered animals and we wanted to share our research with other people. If enough people know and care about the animals, they might be taken off the endangered species list forever. We hope that our book inspires people to care about the future of all wildlife.

Last, each student who wishes to design a cover for the ark submits it for peer review. Matthew's artwork is chosen for the final product.

While assembling our book, Sean suggests that we send a copy to Arnosky. His idea is immediately endorsed. I suggest that we make a video presentation of our *Animal Ark*. The students are excited to participate. We send Arnosky a video in which each student reads one fact from his or her report, along with a copy of the class book and a letter that I've written to explain our project.

I chose the Northern Virginia Flying Squirrel because it's unique and I don't want it to become extinct. Flying squirrels often like to find homes in large forests. They like oak trees and pine trees. To the Northern Virginia Flying Squirrel predators are one reason it's endangered. People are also destroying their habitats by taking away trees. I think that the Northern Virginia Flying Squirrel is a cool little animal.

FIGURE 4–7   *An entry from the class book* Animal Ark

There is a great sense of accomplishment when this project is completed. Each student has contributed to the creation of the *Animal Ark* book and video; the end result exceeds any of our expectations. Why? When the *Animal Ark* project began, I envisioned a brief report as the end product. But as my students became more invested in researching and writing about their animals, they took ownership of the project and offered suggestions for expanding it. They campaigned to take this writing assignment to the next level—publishing a class book that would be shared with Arnosky. As a result, they produced quality work, knowing that not only would other students in the school see their efforts but also Arnosky himself.

All About Arnosky: Team Biographies

Our author study has come full circle. We began by making inferences about Arnosky and then posting hunches on our tree. In today's lesson, we will discover which of our speculations are true. I hand each student a sentence strip that contains a biographical fact (see the author profile on pages 82–84). I then create a semantic map on the board, placing Jim Arnosky's name in a circle in the middle of the board. As students take turns reading their facts, I paraphrase the information, placing it with related information on offshoots from the circle, without telling them what the categories are. For example, I record that Arnosky tends beehives, grows his own food, and spins his own yarn in one section of the map. After we have read and recorded all the facts on the chart paper, I ask the class to figure out a heading for each category of information. The children offer apt headings, such as "Facts About Arnosky's Life"; "Arnosky's Hobbies"; and "Arnosky's Books."

We then return to our hunch tree to confirm, reject, or put on hold our ideas about Arnosky. For example, we affirm that his love for animals began as a child as well as his love of drawing animals in nature. We talk about what to do with hunches that have been rejected and decide to take them off the tree. For hunches about which we have no information, we put these leaves in a pile on the "ground" with the hope of doing further investigation.

We have come to admire this man who has moved us with his devotion to the natural world:

> Over the last twenty years, I have developed an intimate relationship with my subject matter. Through my study of nature I have become convinced that every little thing is part of some whole and that if you look closely enough, you will recognize the scheme of things. You may even find a place for yourself in that order. I have found my place. It is outdoors near the earth, and its waters, near the birds and the beasts. (Collier and Nakamura, 1993, 112)

The next day I mention that it is a shame that there is no published biography about Arnosky. Brian follows my lead and replies, "Maybe we can write one!"

"That's a great idea, Brian," I respond. "We read and talked about biographies earlier this year, so I think we're ready for the challenge."

Jim Arnosky

Born:	September 1, 1946, in New York, New York
Careers:	author, illustrator, wildlife videographer
Awards:	Christopher Medal, Orbis Pictus Honor, ALA Gordon Award, and Outstanding Science Book awards from National Science Teachers Association
Home:	South Ryegate, Vermont

A naturalist, self-taught writer and artist, and award-winning author of more than ninety nature books for children, Jim Arnosky presents an enthusiasm for nature and discovery to young readers through his accurate illustrations and attention to detail. Jim Arnosky started keeping a journal about wildlife encounters when he was a freelance illustrator. He wrote his first children's books in response to the outbreak of Lyme disease which caused many people to fear spending time outdoors. Although his books do advise precautions for exploring outdoors, they emphasize the wonder and excitement of natural discoveries. Arnosky often chooses topics for his books by exploring the wildlife around his Vermont home. He also travels to other parts of the country to observe and learn about animals and habitats where his readers live. In 2005, Jim Arnosky was the recipient of the Lifetime Achievement Key Award for Excellence in Science Books presented by the American Association for the Advancement of Science (AAAS). Arnosky was recognized in the category of Children's Science Books—Illustrator. He also maintains his own website, where he keeps his readers informed of his most recent works and travels.

Arnosky on Arnosky: Quotes About His Life

On his hobbies as a child: "As a child, I lived in rural Pennsylvania and would spend entire days outdoors. I was fascinated with cartoons and wanted to be an artist, so I'd create animal characters, like raccoons and foxes" (Horak 1998, 1).

On how his interest in nature began: "I saw these raccoons at the Central Park Zoo, which I later learned were native to Pennsylvania. It was such a revelation, that these animals lived where I lived even though I couldn't readily see them. I became consumed by the elusive nature of wildlife and began looking for tracks and other signs of life to discover what else lived in my world" (Horak 1998, 1).

On artists and writers who have influenced him: "John Burroughs, John Muir, and Ernest Thomas Seton affected me deeply. Reading Burroughs was like listening to me talk to myself. It felt like I was actually with him on his fishing and hiking expeditions" (Horak 1998, 2).

On becoming an artist: "I had no formal art training but learned a great deal from my father, a skilled patent draftsman" (Holtze 1983, 12–13).

On his lifestyle: "I live in Northern Vermont. My wife Deanna and I have two daughters, Michelle and Amber. We grow all our own food, keep bees for honey, and raise sheep for wool, which Deanna spins into yarn for sweaters, hats, and gloves. We also eat lamb and mutton from our own efforts" (Holtze, 1983, 12–13).

On his hobbies as an adult: "I am an avid fisherman. I enjoy walking, gardening, farming, and canoeing" (Holtze 1983, 12–13).

Arnosky on Arnosky: Quotes About His Writing Process

On when he began writing: "I was a freelance illustrator for *Ranger Rick* and other publications when I met a wise old man who gave me a piece of invaluable advice—keep a journal. I began writing about every wildlife encounter that I had. Writing books, though, came much later" (Horak 1998, 1–2).

On his first book: "In 1974, I wrote the first book about Crinkleroot, the sage woodsman. I wanted him to be an expert in the natural world, yet lovable and whimsical enough to bring natural history to kids. The book was entitled, *I Was Born in a Tree and Raised by Bees.* Recently I re-colorized the art, made the book more current, and it will be published as *Crinkleroot's Nature Almanac*" (Horak 1998, 2).

On where he gets ideas for his books: "Everything comes either from what I see—either through my eyes, a camera, or a video camera—or where I identify a lack of information. I want to know not only what lives where I live, but also where my readers live" (Horak 1998, 2).

On how long it takes him to write and illustrate a book: "I do four books a year, and each takes about three months" (Horak 1998, 2).

On his writing process: "First I research a site, photographing or videotaping a species. Then I let the ideas percolate for a while before I illustrate my images. The pictures determine the story, so the words actually come last" (Horak 1998, 2).

On where he does his work: "I do much of my writing in our living room and I do my drawing in a room set aside for drawing in the center of our home" (Holtze 1983, 12–13).

Biographical References

Arnosky, J. No date. "Jim Arnosky's Biography." Retrieved May 3, 2006, from http://www.jimarnosky.com/biography.html.

———. No date. "Jim Arnosky Honored for Lifetime Contribution to Science" Retrieved May 3, 2006 from http://www.jimarnosky.com/award.html.

Children's Literature. 2005. "Meet Authors and Illustrators: Jim Arnosky." Retrieved May 3, 2006, from www.childrenslit.com/f_arnosk.htm.

Collier, A. and J. Nakamura, eds. 1993. "Arnosky, Jim 1946–." In *Major Authors and Illustrators for Children and Young Adults: A Selection of Sketches from Something About the Author,* 111–114. Detroit: Gale Research.

Horak, L. 1998. "Talking Turkey and Then Some: A Naturalist Brings the Wild World to Children." Retrieved May 3, 2006, from www.bookpage.com/9811bp/jim_arnosky.html.

Holtze, S. H., ed. 1983. "Jim Arnosky." In *Fifth Book of Junior Authors and Illustrators,* 12–13. New York: H. W. Wilson.

Jim Arnosky Books Used During this Author Study

Arnosky, J. 1993. *Crinkleroot's Guide to Walking in Wild Places.* New York: Aladdin.

———. 1992a. *Crinkleroot's Guide to Knowing the Birds.* New York: Simon and Schuster.

———. 1992b. *Crinkleroot's Guide to Knowing the Trees.* New York: Simon and Schuster.

———. 1994. *All About Alligators.* New York: Scholastic.

———. 1996a. *All About Deer.* New York: Scholastic.

———. 1996b. *Crinkleroot's Guide to Knowing Butterflies and Moths.* New York: Simon and Schuster.

———. 1997a. *Crinkleroot's Guide to Knowing Animal Habitats.* New York: Simon and Schuster.

———. 1997b. *Rabbits and Raindrops.* New York: Putnam.

———. 1998a. *All About Turkeys.* New York: Scholastic.

———. 1998b. *Crinkleroot's Visit to Crinkle Cove.* New York: Aladdin.

———. 1999a. *All About Owls.* New York: Scholastic.

———. 1999b. *Arnosky's Ark.* Washington, D.C.: National Geographic.

———. 2000a. *All About Turtles.* New York: Scholastic.

———. 2000b. *Rattlesnake Dance.* New York: G. P. Putnam's Sons.

———. 2002a. *All About Frogs.* New York: Scholastic.

———. 2002b. *All About Rattlesnakes.* New York: Scholastic.

———. 2003. *All About Sharks.* New York: Scholastic.

As momentum builds, we brainstorm how we might organize Arnosky's biography. Recognizing that we have limited information (e.g., we don't know much about his childhood), I redirect them to the previous day's semantic map. Danielle suggests that we use the same headings of information (life facts, his books, and his hobbies) for our biography. I then divide students into eight groups of three. The trios meet and decide who will write which of these three designated paragraphs. Each child drafts his biographical contribution, applying what he has learned about paragraph construction and paraphrasing with teacher support. Group members then peer revise and edit each other's work before submitting it to a teacher for a final edit. We are impressed with their efforts and enthusiasm.

Next, group members work to assemble and finalize their biographies. They create illustrations that correspond to their paragraphs. Several groups decide that they would like to have an author page. These students glue their individual school pictures on this final page; some write two to three sentences about themselves. In addition, some groups decide that although Arnosky often does not use a table of contents, they'll include one in their book.

Finally, after brainstorming titles, we settle on *All About Arnosky*. Groups then create a cover for their book and bind the pages together using the school's binding machine. Figure 4–8 showcases the biography written by Joseph and his peers. After exchanging and enjoying these biographies, we add them to the biography book basket in our classroom library.

As a postscript to this section on biographical response, I later found an excellent website authored by Arnosky. *Jim Arnosky's Outdoor Journal* (www.jimarnosky.com/) features a letter from Arnosky inviting readers to visit his travel log, bordered by five photographs. My third graders would have enjoyed reading this travel log as well as accessing Arnosky's related links (list of books, coloring book, Crinkle Corner, etc.). This website also sells *A Video Visit with Jim Arnosky: All About Alligators*, in which Arnosky explains firsthand the research process he used to create his book about alligators.

Concluding Comments

As our author study draws to a close, I ask each child to complete a survey. Matt's completed survey is presented in Figure 4–9. Overall, their feedback on the author study is very positive. Twenty-one of the twenty-four youngsters circle *yes* to the first question in Figure 4–9. To ascertain whether they think an author study in general is a good idea, I examine their responses to item 7. In addition to Matt's indirect but energetic endorsement of author studies in this item, eleven others think that reading the books of one author is worthwhile. For example, Joseph writes: "I like to study one author because Jim Arnosky's books can be very enjoyable to read. Also the projects are fun." Four others also note the fun projects. Six mention an intrigue with the author as person. For example, Thomas writes: "I think doing an author study is a good idea because you get to learn about their life. Also, because you can see what kind of person that author is."

In examining the dissenting votes to item 7, two others agree with Matt that one author isn't enough. As Jonathan astutely puts it: "You should study more [authors] to learn the difference of the authors." Danielle is the only third grader to express reluctance about the author study. Her response to item 7 is as follows: "I do not think it is [a good idea to study books of one author] because we should read other books." In responding to item 8 in Figure 4–9, she confesses that she is "tired of reading the Jim

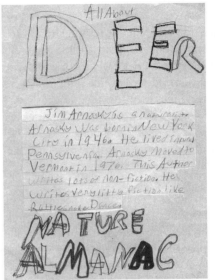

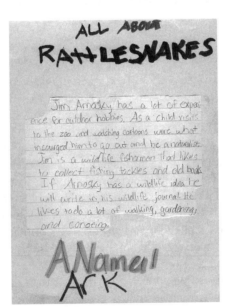

(continued)

FIGURE 4–8   One group's Arnosky biography

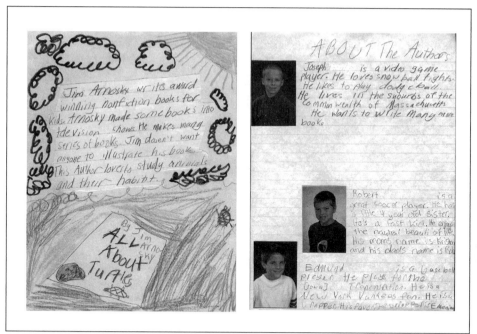

Figure 4–8 *(Continued)*

Arnosky books." Danielle's comments make me realize the importance of soliciting feedback at an earlier point in an author study so that I can make adjustments to accommodate the range of interests and abilities. I suspect that Danielle, an advanced reader and writer, may have found Arnosky's All About books too simple. In hindsight, for example, I could have gauged Danielle's interest in accessing, reading, and reporting on Arnosky's websites, which are written at a more advanced level, and invited her to become our classroom expert on Arnosky.

Overall, my third graders' enthusiastic response to this author study assure me that author studies afford opportunities, in Matt's words, "to read well together, learn together, and have fun together."

Several weeks after we finished our author study, I receive an envelope that is addressed to my class and has a stamp of a sleeping fox in the upper left-hand corner. When I turn the envelope over, my heart skips a beat as I stare at the label: ARNOSKY, South Ryegate, VT. I tear open the envelope and read the reply (see Figure 4–10). While my students are at recess, I photocopy the letter and place one copy on each desk. Upon arrival, their excitement is uncontainable. It is as if Jim Arnosky is standing right there in the classroom with us. I couldn't have imagined a better ending to our school year.

Name: *Matthew*   Number: _____

JIM ARNOSKY AUTHOR STUDY SURVEY

1. Did you enjoy studying the books of Jim Arnosky?   (Yes)   No

2. What was the best part about studying Jim Arnosky's books?

My favorite part was doing the all about arnosky books because I like writing assignments.

3. Read each of the activities (listed below) that we did while studying Jim Arnosky. Write number 1 next to your most favorite activity. Write number 2 next to your second favorite activity. Write number 3 next to your third favorite activity.

_2_ listening to/reading books   _____ unpacking the suitcase

_____ creating a friend for Crinkleroot   _____ writing 5 frog facts

_1_ writing ALL About Arnosky   _____ making a table of contents

_____ writing a book review   _____ filling out the animal profile sheet

_____ sharing a memory of a time you encountered a frog

_3_ choosing an animal to include in your own animal ark

_____ participating in literature circles for Crinkleroot books

_____ doing the rattlesnake dance

4. Was there any part of the author study that you didn't like? Tell what you didn't like and why?

The part I didn't like was the Crinkleroot literature circles I didn't like that because I didn't find Crinkleroot books very fasinating.

(continued)

FIGURE 4–9   *Matt's survey on the author study*

5. Place a star next to your favorite Jim Arnosky book. Place a check next to your second favorite book. Place a circle next to your third favorite book.

_____ Crinkleroot's Guide to Walking in Wild Places
_____ Crinkelroot's Nature Almanac
_____ Crinkleroot's Guide to Knowing the Trees
_____ Crinkleroot's Guide to Knowing the Birds
_____ Crinkleroot's Guide to Knowing Butterflies and Moths
_____ Crinkleroot's Guide to Knowing Animal Habitats
_____ Crinklroot's Visit to Crinkle Cove

★ Arnosky's Ark   _____ The Rattlesnake Dance
_____ All About Turtles   _____ All About Turkeys
_____ All About Deer   ○ All About Frogs
✓ All About Owls   _____ All About Alligators

6. Why is the book with the star next to it your favorite?

The book with the star next to it is my favorite because I liked learning about indangered species

7. Do you think it is a good idea to study books of one author? Yes (No)
Why? Give 2 reasons if you can.

I think you shouldn't study one auther because it's not enough you should do 5 authers because you wouldn't learn enough by studying one auther.

8. If you happen to notice a new Jim Arnosky book in a library or in a bookstore, will you pick it up and read it? (Yes) No
Tell why or why not?

I would read it because I like Jim Arnosky's book because he writes nature books and I like nature and learning about it.

9. If you had to give one piece of advice to teacher about doing author studies, what would you tell them?

I would tell a teacher teach kids to read well together, learn together and have fun together.

FIGURE 4–9   (Continued)

May 22, 2004

Dear Miss Harris and your third grade class,

Deanna and I watched your video this morning and we enjoyed every minute of it. I was especially touched by the fact that it was dedicated to me. I feel honored.

The selection of animals was very broadly based. It's good to know we have young people caring about these endangered species. In Vermont, our Peregrine Falcons and Ospreys have made a good comeback. God I believe the Bald Eagle is next to make a strong return to our rivers and hills.

Presently I am working on a story about Buffalo. Deanna and I followed their tracks in the Witchita Mountains in southern Oklahoma, and in the northeastern part of the state where the tall grass prairie is preserved. The scientific name for these animals is Bison. But I call them Buffalo.

When I began making books about American wildlife some 30 years ago, I never imagined my work would inspire so many people to write and draw their own books about their own favorite animals. Thank you so much for sharing your work with me.

Jim Arnosky

FIGURE 4–10   *Letter from Jim Arnosky*

5

Fritzing Through History: Jean Fritz
Grade 3

Maryanne Lally and Carol Brennan Jenkins

One January morning, my (Maryanne) third graders arrive to find a bulletin board that contains a large photograph of a young Jean Fritz steering a boat on the Yangtse River. The accompanying speech bubble reads:

> I was born in Hankow, China in 1915. I moved to America when I was thirteen years old.

A world map is displayed next to this speech bubble; arrows point to Hankow and to Massachusetts, labeled respectively: "Jean Fritz was born here" and "You are here."

As the third graders gather around, spontaneous conversation begins. Hayley asks, "Who is Jean Fritz? Why does she live in China?"

While placing a number of Fritz's books on the table to the side of the bulletin board, I explain that Jean Fritz is an author whose work I greatly admire and that we will be enjoying some of her books as we study colonial Massachusetts. I briefly recount Fritz's early life in China, explaining that her parents were missionaries and that she attended a British school in Hankow. I then post the following speech bubble next to Fritz's picture:

> I was bullied by a Scottish boy in school because I was an American.

I read the bullying excerpt from Fritz's autobiography, *Homesick*, in which Fritz writes, "I went to a British school and every morning we sang, 'God save the King.' Of course the British children loved singing about their gracious king" (1982, 10). As an American, though, Fritz resented this mandate and one day refused to sing, announcing to her teacher, "It is not my national anthem" (11). During recess, Ian Forbes, a Scottish boy, tried to force Fritz to say, "God save the king," by stomping on her foot. Defiant, Fritz shot back, "Why should I? Americans haven't said that since George the Third" (12). As Forbes twisted her arm, Fritz whispered, "I'll never say it" (12).

My third graders are indignant:

AARON: She was bullied by a Scottish boy? That's not fun! Just being an American in China doesn't mean you're different! Is that why she moved?

EMILY: I feel very bad for her. I do not want to be her if she was getting bullied.

JOHN: I think that Scottish boy should not of bullied Jean Fritz because it matters what is inside, not outside and she probably got her feelings hurt.

As the class continues to rally to Fritz's defense, we discuss why bullies do what they do and how we can stop them. I then tell the class that tomorrow we will begin our journey through Fritz's biographies. And who better to start with than King George, the culprit himself!

I have launched my author study (the original draft was coplanned with colleague Kristen Simonds), confident that I've spurred an interest in this acclaimed writer. Over the course of this study, I continue to fill this bulletin board with quotes and/or information about Jean Fritz, with the goal of showing my third graders how life experiences shape a writer. A photograph of the bulletin board at the end of the study is presented in Figure 5–1. Biographical response is just one strand highlighted in this chapter. In addition, I use Fritz's masterfully crafted biographies to usher my third graders into the history of the American Revolution, to evoke personal responses about the lives of key historical figures, and to extend their understanding of the genre

FIGURE 5–1   *Fritz bulletin board*

of biography, specifically the elements of characterization, chronology, and literary devices such as repetition and humor. The curriculum map in Appendix A presents the highlights of author study events and corresponding local and national standards (Massachusetts Curriculum Frameworks [ELA and social studies] and IRA/NCTE Standards for the English Language Arts).

My Classroom

I teach third grade in a K–8 elementary school in a middle-class town on Cape Cod. In order to accommodate the range of literacy abilities, I implement a guided reading program (Fountas and Pinnell 2001). My ten girls and ten boys read a wide variety of genres and learn the strategies and skills that effective readers and writers use. Each day, during the one-and-a-half-hour block for guided reading, I conduct a whole-group minilesson or shared reading and then meet with leveled groups. Writing work-shop follows; students choose their own writing topics, write at their own pace, and meet with me to confer on their drafts. Our Title I reading teacher also spends time in my classroom, assessing needs and teaching small groups and individuals.

Author Study in Action

Like many teachers, I find that the most effective manner of getting everything done is to integrate content and skills across the reading and social studies blocks. Therefore, this author study often flowed from a morning reading lesson to an afternoon social studies block. The Massachusetts Curriculum Frameworks specify that students learn Massachusetts history and the Revolutionary War in third grade. What better way to introduce third graders to this pivotal period in history than through Jean Fritz's biographies of the Founding Fathers and others, which have earned much acclaim:

> In her biographies Fritz attempts to get at the truth of the individual through his likes, dislikes, worries, joys, successes, failures. In each case she reveals the humanity of this individual, presenting his life as revealed in his diary, letters, and other original sources. Through her humorous style she paints a full, believable picture of each individual, using specific, exact language and precise detail. (Busbin, 1986, p. 163)

Personal Responses to Can't You Make Them Behave, King George?

Displaying the front cover of *Can't You Make Them Behave, King George?* (1976), I read the title and ask, "To whom is Jean Fritz referring to when she writes *them* in the title?"
Many children reply, "The colonists."
I add, "Who do you think is asking King George this question?"
Mikey suggests, "Maybe the king was asking it to himself, or maybe the Redcoats."
Aaron adds, "Maybe the officers in the army or tax collectors."
I agree that these are excellent possibilities; I am pleased that our previous lessons on the American Revolution have taken hold. I remind Mikey and his peers that not

all colonists wanted to be free of the king's rule; perhaps it was the Tories who were asking this question, or perhaps the English people themselves.

I ask what we call a book that is written about a person's life. Hands fly; the students chorally respond, "Biography!" At the beginning of the year, they wrote autobiographies that served as a community-building activity. The distinction between autobiography and biography was made concrete when I asked them to write a biography of an elderly family member or elderly friend or neighbor. They helped generate the questions they would ask in an interview; I guided them to focus on the life chronology. They audiotaped these interviews and collected photographs. They chose how they wanted to portray their person; some created life quilts, others assembled scrapbooks with captions, and so forth. The culminating project was a presentation of the biographies at a reception for guests of honor and family members. These activities set the stage to meet the reigning queen of biography, Jean Fritz.

As with most of the biographies introduced in this author study, I encourage personal response as a starting point to the literature. The King George biography is a natural for such response. Fritz elicits laughter and groans as the children sympathize with young George whose "teachers nagged him about being lazy" because he "daydreamed and sometimes drew pictures on the margins of his schoolbooks" (1996, 7). For example:

> EMILY: I at least have to daydream ten times a day! If I didn't daydream a lot one day, I would daydream like thirty times the next day. I always stare at something beautiful and daydream.
>
> MELISSA: I daydream a lot too. I daydream about playing soccer and winning the game but it's not true because we only won one game.

Of course, even when I'm focusing on personal response, other types of responses find their way into the conversation. For example, Ryan notes about George's daydreaming, "That is cool—he's like me. How does she [Fritz] know these things?"

"Great question, Ryan." I explain that historians access primary sources, such as diaries and letters adding that maybe someday their journals might be a source for *their* biography! I note that we will discuss Fritz's research process and sources more fully at a later point but add that Fritz confesses to daydreaming when she was in school:

> Sure I did. I daydreamed a lot. Probably that was one reason I didn't do so well in math. I just daydreamed through it. It's not a good idea! (Scholastic n.d.b)

What Makes a Good Biography? Text Analysis of Can't You Make Them Behave, King George?

The following day, I ask my third graders to help me list the characteristics of a good biography. I record their ideas, elaborating as we go and adding my own:

- tells the story of a person's life, often in chronological order (birth, childhood, etc.)
- includes episodes such as obstacles and achievements in the chronology

- makes the person believable by showing both strengths and weaknesses
- weaves facts together to make the story interesting and enjoyable
- is based on facts collected from many sources (interviews, diaries, letters, photographs, historical records)

I then organize small groups and explain that their job is to give Fritz a thumbs-up or thumbs-down on each item, after discussing evidence in *Can't You Make Them Behave, King George?* I give each team a copy of the book and the list of biography criteria. Fritz earns a thumbs-up on all accounts; they are able to justify their votes with specifics from the biography. For example, Esther notes that a biography she is reading during independent reading is "just facts about the person, not information about their personality like Jean Fritz does."

Others also note that what sets Fritz's books apart is her use of funny details. I explain this humor from Fritz's (n.d.a) perspective:

> I get letters from readers sometimes who say they like the way I add "fun" to history. I don't add anything. It's all true, because the past times were just as filled with exciting events and "fun" stories as are present times.

We talk about the effect of humor on the reader; I ask whether they think they will find humor in other Fritz biographies. They are confident they will. John suggests that we add humor to our list of criteria; all agree.

What Are Personal Traits? Text Analysis of George Washington's Mother

Characterization is a central feature of an effective biography (Huck, Hepler, and Hickman 1987; Cullinan and Galda 1994). Biographers strive to make readers care about their subjects, by revealing "a real human being with both shortcomings and virtues" (Huck, Hepler, and Hickman 1987, 571). Biographers must not only stay true to historical fact but also select and arrange facts to provide a truthful portrayal. A starting point for children in understanding biographical characterization is the distinction between fact and opinion, another mandated curriculum skill. To introduce this distinction, I ask, "If someone was going to write a book about me, what kind of information would she need?" I ask them to describe me as if they were telling a stranger about me, other than my physical appearance. As they offer ideas, I record specifics on a chart under two columns, "Facts" and "Personal Traits." Under "Facts," I record dates, times, names, and so forth. As they generate ideas about my likes, dislikes, and behaviors, I log them under the "Personal Traits."

John then astutely inquires, "So, personal trait information is like an opinion?"

I explain that personal traits, also called character traits, are opinions that are based on factual observations garnered over time. I then point to the posted two-column chart and challenge them to listen for the two types of information as I read Fritz's book, *George Washington's Mother* (1992a). I stop to demonstrate both types early in the read-aloud, and then I ask the children to snap their fingers when they hear information that should be recorded on the chart. Opinions range from "She was selfish," and "She was self-centered," to "She doesn't want George to get hurt," and "She was loving and caring." I ask for the facts to support their opinions, that a person can be loving and selfish at the same time. Fritz's content is so detailed that they do this with ease. We discuss how these characteristics are revealed through Mary Washington's words and actions. I then give each child a blank copy of this two-column chart and a sheet that contains excerpts from the book. I direct them to work with a partner to read each item and glue it under the correct heading. As Figure 5–2 reveals, most of my third graders successfully distinguish between the two concepts.

Chronology: The Text Structure That Typifies Biography

With an introduction to characterization, we are ready to examine the text structure that often characterizes biographies: chronology. By third grade, children are fairly proficient at comprehending the text structure of chronology (Englert and Hiebert, 1984). Such awareness is evident when I ask, "If you were going to write a biography about a person, where would you begin?"

Hayley states, "I would start at the beginning of their life."

Everyone concurs until I mention *George Washington's Mother*. "Where did Jean Fritz begin Mary Washington's story?"

Maddie notes, "When she was grown up."

I reread the opening page of *George Washington's Mother* and confirm Maddie's observation. Unlike King George's biography, which begins with his childhood and moves chronologically through his life, Mary Washington's biography begins when she is a young woman. We speculate on why Fritz didn't include Mary's childhood. Perhaps there are no accurate historical records. Perhaps few interesting things happened to young Mary so Fritz didn't include her childhood. We then ponder what Fritz said about this biography:

> I make it come alive for me. If it's alive for me, it's going to be alive for children. I think I try to find the details that are interesting and appeal to children. When I wrote about Washington's mother, there were so many details. (Scholastic n.d.b)

With further discussion, we hypothesize that Fritz had so many stories about young Mary and her famous son that she didn't have room in the book to include her childhood. I then briefly explain that publishers limit the number of pages that can be included in a book. I reinforce the challenge that Fritz and other biographers face when forced to select information about their subject. I then piggyback this with another Fritz quote to help them begin to understand that the selection of facts must first and foremost advance the story, keeping the chronology in sight but not slavishly so:

> Although my framework is chronological, I don't feel bound by chronology. I can begin a series of sentences with "once" or "sometimes," listing events regardless of their sequence. I know that in the end the book will assume the shape of a story, not because it has been forced or coaxed into that, but because the story is already there.

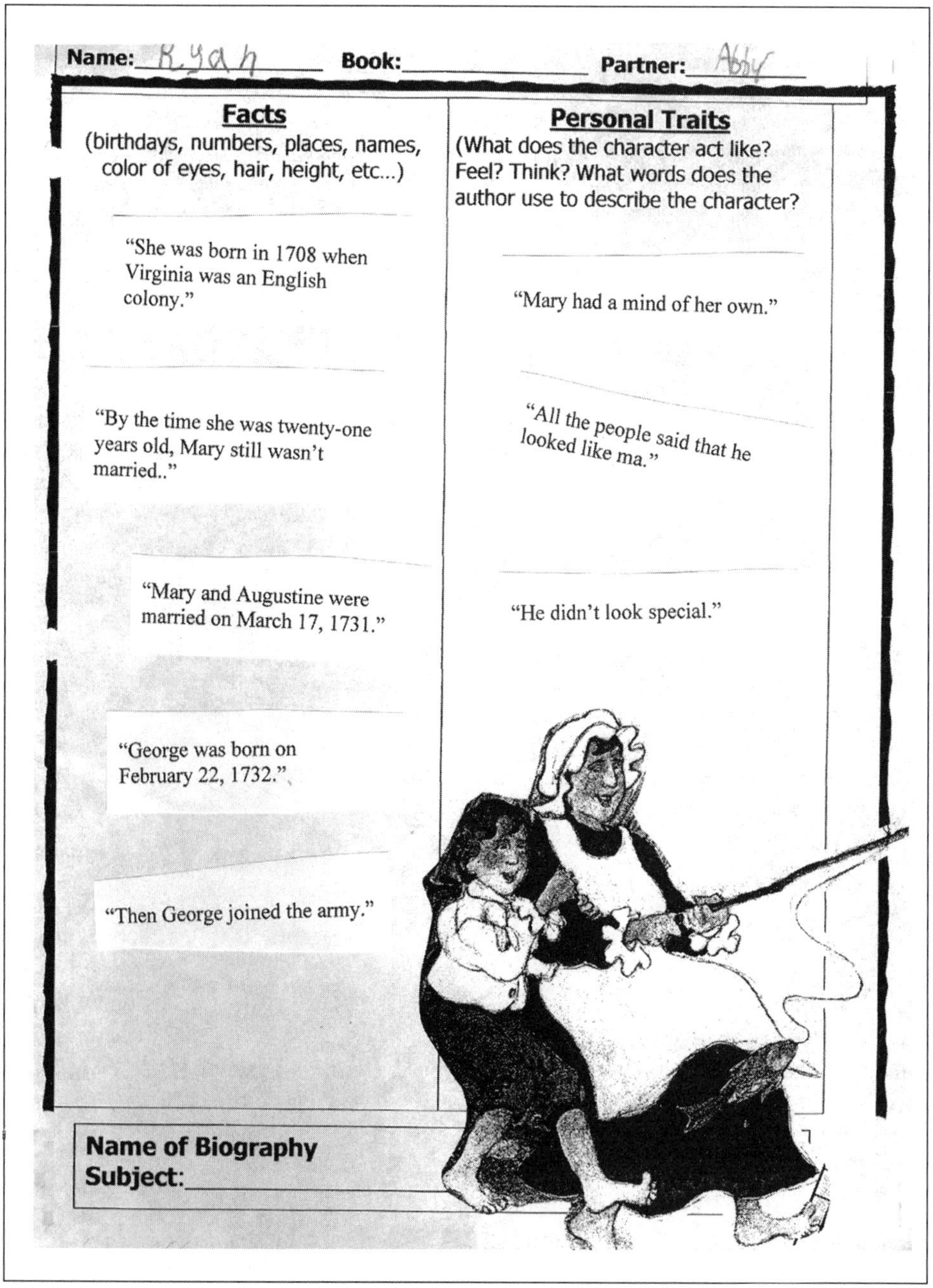

Name: R.yah   **Book:** _____   **Partner:** Abby

Facts
(birthdays, numbers, places, names, color of eyes, hair, height, etc...)

"She was born in 1708 when Virginia was an English colony."

"By the time she was twenty-one years old, Mary still wasn't married.."

"Mary and Augustine were married on March 17, 1731."

"George was born on February 22, 1732."

"Then George joined the army."

Personal Traits
(What does the character act like? Feel? Think? What words does the author use to describe the character?

"Mary had a mind of her own."

"All the people said that he looked like ma."

"He didn't look special."

Name of Biography Subject: _____

FIGURE 5–2   *Facts and traits from* George Washington's Mother

Every person is a story. And when a writer lives with a character, the story line emerges, gradually becoming more distinct, until at last it takes command. (1990, 29)

We then return to *George Washington's Mother* to determine the degree to which it is chronologically ordered. After a quick picture walk using time-order words such as *first, then, next,* and *finally,* we conclude that while this biography starts at a later point in life, it unfolds chronologically.

I then organize the class into groups and challenge: "If I give each group a set of sentence strips that talk about Paul Revere's life, do you think you can put them in the right chronology or sequence? These sentences are from another Fritz biography called *And Then What Happened, Paul Revere?*—a book that we haven't read yet. But I think you have a good enough understanding about how the text structure of chronology works that you will be able to order these strips."

They dive into the activity, spreading the color-coded strips on the rug and debating the order. Discussion about key time-order words, dates, and other clues accompany their decision making. For sets that do not contain obvious clues, active rereading and further debating occurs. Upon completion, I ask each group to chorally read its strips in order; when an order is challenged, the class works to arrive at a consensus. Then, standing in a large circle, we arrange the sets in sequential order with each group articulating its reasoning. Ultimate confirmation of their work is at hand. I pass out copies of *And Then What Happened, Paul Revere?* (1973) and the third graders settle in to listen to Jean Fritz (1973) read her award-winning biography. I stop and start the tape so that groups can verify the order of their strips or make changes on the time line of Paul Revere's very busy life.

We end this two-day session with a discussion about how an understanding of text structure helps us both comprehend and compose nonfiction texts.

Elements of a Chronology: Paul Revere and Hula Hoops

I work to extend the students' understanding that biography is not a mere string of events in a person's life. Once again, I use my own life to reinforce familiar concepts and to illustrate new concepts. I draw a circle on the board and write my name in the middle. I then draw five spokes, each ending with a circle and containing one of the following labels: "Personal Facts" (birth date, places, etc.), "Personal Traits" (shy, kind, etc.), "Important Influences" (people, events), "Obstacles" (hardships, difficulties faced), and "Accomplishments." I then read examples from my life and have them help me place the information in the correct category.

It is now their turn to do the same. I give each child five tongue depressors and ask them to write personal information that they are willing to share with the class relating to each category. While they are working, I place five hula hoops on the rug to replicate the web on the board. Each hoop contains one of the category labels. As we gather around the hula hoops, I ask volunteers to read and place their stick in the correct hula hoop. Others then add theirs. Because we have already explored the categories of personal facts and personal traits, we concentrate on the categories of obstacles, achievements, and influences (see Figure 5–3). The third graders listen attentively and respectfully to peers; I informally assess their understanding of the categories and reteach when appropriate.

I then explain that when Fritz is researching a subject, she pays particular attention to the details that exemplify each of these categories (when applicable) because she wants to make readers care about her subjects. We care about people who endure hardships, who work hard to achieve something important, and who acknowledge others who supported or aided their efforts. I reinforce that a good biography is not a mere collection of facts; it represents careful selection of facts that bring the character to life, that make him or her human.

I could have extended this activity as follows: Ask eight children to come to the front of the room and hang signs around their necks. Each sign contains an event from Paul Revere's life; students stand in scrambled order. Examples of signs, minus the page numbers and categories, include:

- Paul's father dies; Paul works extra jobs to earn money for family. (p. 8) [Obstacle]
- England taxes the colonies. (p. 17) [Obstacle/Influence]
- Paul defies King George and participates in the Boston Tea Party. (p. 19) [Achievement]

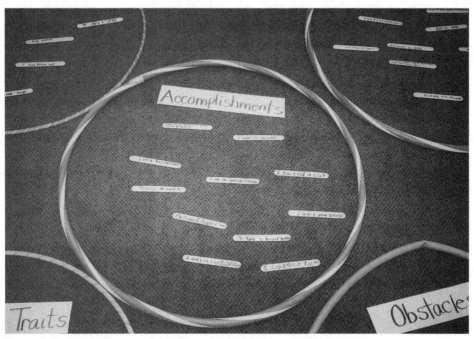

FIGURE 5–3 *The students sorted their biographical information into categories*

- British invade the colonies. (p. 25) [Influence]
- Paul rides to warn colonists. (p. 33) [Achievement]
- Paul is captured by British soldiers. (p. 34) [Obstacle]

Ask the audience to read the signs chorally and then to sequence the events, checking against the book. Distribute strips labeled "Obstacles," "Influences," and so on to pairs in the audience. Working with the six sign people, have them decide which events match their category. Discuss the overlap of categories as they debate, for example, whether taxation should be classified as an obstacle or an influence, concluding perhaps that the taxes were both a hardship for the colonists as well as a catalyst for the revolution. Ask whether they think Fritz had to decide which category to label each event or whether she just had to be sure to include it. Reassemble the chronology; have each team justify its match(es). With students standing around the room with signs in chronological order, ask whether Fritz put all of the obstacles that Revere faced in one section of the book; repeat with achievements. Conclude that Fritz integrated these categories of information, when applicable, as they occurred across a person's life.

Biographical Insights About Jean Fritz

Recall that each morning of the author study begins with a speech bubble about Jean Fritz (see Figure 5–1). As previously noted, initial biographical data focuses on Fritz's early life in China, and later information focuses on her new life in America. For example, the class is amazed that Fritz had no idea what the Pledge of Allegiance was:

> "What Pledge of Allegiance?" So she [Fritz's aunt] explained that every morning we'd start off by pledging allegiance to the flag and she taught me how to say it, my hand over my heart. After that, I practiced every day while I was feeding the chickens. I'd clap my hand over my heart and tell them about "one nation indivisible." (Fritz 1982, 145)

As the author study evolves, the speech bubbles also include information about Fritz as a writer. For example, a picture of Fritz placing a book manuscript in the refrigerator and the following speech bubble trigger energized talk:

> Every winter I take three weeks off from my writing to go to Virgin Gorda, an island in the Caribbean Sea, where I swim and snorkel and just stare at the wonderful blue-green water. I leave the manuscript I'm working on at home, but that's scary! Suppose the house should burn down! So, before I go out of town, I put my manuscript in the safest place I can think of—the refrigerator. Then off I go. (Fritz 1992, 20)

We discuss Fritz's writing process in general:

> My beat may lie in another time, but my approach is that of a reporter, trying for a scoop, looking for clues, connecting facts, digging under the surface. History is full of gossip; it's real people and emotion. (Houghton Mifflin n.d.)

We also discuss her insights specific to particular books. For example, after we read *And Then What Happened, Paul Revere?* we talk about her approach to writing this biography:

> In my so-called younger biographies . . . I zero in on the main characteristic of my subject. This immediately puts the reader on a familiar footing with the character, and it gives me a chance to match my narrative voice to the thrust of the material. Paul Revere for instance, was one of the compulsively busy, active men, into everything, rushing from one project to another. So I assume a rather breathless style for his story—short sentences, long accumulated sentences that race from comma to comma, broken phrases, questions to move the story along quickly. (Fritz 1990, 28)

Along with the Founding Fathers, Jean Fritz is capturing our hearts and minds.

Language Play in Fritz's Biographies

Fritz's *Why Don't You Get a Horse, Sam Adams?* (1974) delights the third graders. They are amazed that such a famous and brave patriot was afraid to ride a horse, empathizing as they share some of their fears while enjoying the humor of his predicament.

The next day, I hold up the book and ask what they notice about the book title. Jackson notes that the title is repeated throughout the text. I ask why they think Fritz uses repetition. Melissa replies that maybe Fritz is using repetition like the fairy tale writers do. I am pleased that they recall many of the repetitious and memorable lines (e.g., "Fee, fi, fo, fum . . . !" and "I'll huff and I'll puff . . . !") in the fairy tales we studied earlier in the year. We then talk about how this stylistic device serves to keep our interest in Sam Adams while we learn about his role in the American Revolution.

I then share that Fritz found this line in an actual letter that Sam's cousin and second president of the United States, John Adams, had written to James Warren, a fellow patriot, about Sam's lack of equestrian skills (Fritz 1974). Fritz's use of a familiar primary source document is of great interest to the children.

I then ask if they notice how the Sam Adams title compares with that of others we've read, showing previous books. They are quick to note the question format. I ask if we have encountered Fritz's use of repeated questions in her other books. They recall the line "And then what happened?" in the Paul Revere book and decide that Fritz used this line to emphasize how event-filled Paul Revere's life was. I extend by sharing Fritz's rationale: "All of them [her books] have titles that are in the form of a question because questions imply surprise. We underestimate the power of surprise in education. It seems to me that I have been surprised into learning almost everything I know" (1990, 26).

Would You Care for One Lump or Two? Colonial Tea Party

Our last Fritz biography in the author study is *Will You Sign Here, John Hancock?* (1976). Having already observed the American Revolution played out from various angles in Fritz's previous books, I ask the students to predict what Fritz might include in this biography.

Jean Fritz

Born: November 16, 1915, in Hankow, China

Careers: librarian, teacher, author

Awards: Numerous awards including Newbery Honor Book; American Book Award; New York Times Outstanding Book; Orbis Pictus award; NCTE; American Library Association; Boston Globe–Horn Book Honor Book

Home: Dobbs Ferry, New York

From an early age, Jean Fritz knew that she wanted to be a writer. "The first 13 years of my life I lived in China. My parents were missionaries there, and I was an only child. Often I felt lonely and out of place. Writing for me became my private place, where no one would come" (Fritz n.d.b). In her awarding-winning autobiography, *Homesick: My Own Story* (1982), Fritz recounts the dissonance that underscored her childhood—a love for her birth land, China, but a deep longing for her homeland, America. Fritz attributes her love of her American history to "a subconscious desire to find roots—I felt like a girl without a country" (Fritz n.d.b). This obsession percolated until the 1950s, when she began writing historical fiction, followed by a book for adults about the American Revolution, which triggered the idea for the first of her Founding Fathers biographies, *And Then What Happened, Paul Revere?* (Busbin 1986). These biographies as well as others on historical figures such as Lizzie Stanton, Pocahontas, and Teddy Roosevelt have won her critical acclaim.

Fritz on Fritz: Quotes About Her Childhood

On growing up in China: "The trouble with living on the wrong side of the world was that I didn't feel like a real American. For instance, I could never be president of the United States. I didn't want to be president; I wanted to be a writer. Still, why should there be a law saying that only a person born in the United States could be president? It was as if I wouldn't be American enough" (Fritz 1982, 10).

On her favorite subjects: "English, writing and reading. I was never good in math, and I never liked it. I didn't like the way history was taught—I always suspected there was more there. And there was! I was taught a kind of surface history. But [the] most important thing is to get below the surface, and that's what I like to do in my writing" (Scholastic n.d.b)

On favorite books: "When I lived in China, there were no libraries. My mother bought books for me and they were mostly the classics. I read *Peter Pan*, *The Secret Garden*, the Rosemary books, and Kipling's *Just So Stories* was one of my favorites. No, I didn't read historical fiction. It didn't exist when I was growing up in China. . . . One of the most important things in my childhood were the new books that came in" (Scholastic n.d.b).

Fritz on Fritz: Quotes About Her Writing Process

On where she gets her ideas: "My ideas find me. Ideas for books are a mixture of what comes in from the outside and what you are giving of yourself" (Kovacs and Preller 1991, 98).

On research: "As a biographer, I try to uncover the adventures and personalities behind each character I research. Once my character and I have reached an under-standing, then I begin the detective work—reading old books, old letters, old news-papers, and visiting the places where my subject lived. Often I turn up surprises, and of course, I pass them on" (Scholastic n.d.b).

On drafting: "I don't work from a very detailed outline. As I'm doing the research, the book more or less falls into shape. Then I write a very brief outline of where things are going to fit. . . . When I get started on a book, I get quite obsessive about it. I can't get it out of my mind. I lie awake at night, going over the lines, wondering what's coming next. Most of my creative work is done in those wee hours of the night when I want to be asleep. Things get solved when I am in a kind of going-to-sleep or trying-to-get-to-sleep mood that don't get solved sitting at a desk" (Kovacs and Preller 1991, 98).

On writer's block: "I've never really had writer's block. I've had times when it's dif-ficult to go on. Usually I find the problem is that I need to go back and do more research. I need to go back and find out what I really want to say instead of just ramble. The hardest part is to start a new book" (Scholastic n.d.b).

On revision: "Every morning, I read over everything I've done up to that point. By the law of averages, one would think there would be a certain percentage of sen-tences that would turn out right the first time. None of my mine seem to, though" (Kovacs and Preller 1991, 99).

   "My writing, when you look at the first version, is a mess of crossing out. . . . Last summer I visited Laura Ingalls Wilder's home and saw the original versions of the *Little House* books. She never crossed out a single word, I couldn't believe it" (Scholastic n.d.b).

On favorite part of the writing process: "The research. I love it! I love digging and finding little, out-of-the-way nuggets of information that are funny, amazing, etc. It's the out-of-the-way things that attract me and that I want as part of the book" (Scho-lastic n.d.b).

On length of time to write a book: "It takes about a year. . . . In my books I want to be sure that everything is the way it really happened. When you see quotation marks in any of my books, I only do that if I know that someone has really said it—I don't make it up" (Scholastic n.d.b).

On advice to young writers: "I always tell kids who like to write to keep a diary. It's a place to write things that happen, but also the kinds of feelings they're having. Anybody who wants to write has to be in touch with his or her own feelings. The time to get in touch with them is when you're in school, when you're young" (Kovacs and Preller 1991, 99).

Biographical References

Busbin, O. M. 1986. *Dictionary of Literary Biography, Volume 52: American Writers for Children Since 1960: Fiction.* Detroit: Gale group.

Fritz, J. 1982. *Homesick: My Own Story.* New York: Putnam.

———. No date a. "Jean Fritz." Retrieved August 8, 2004, from www.cbsbooks.org/cbcmagazine/meet/jeanfritz.html.

———. No date b. "Jean Fritz's Biography." Retrieved May 25, 2004, from www.teacher.scholastic.com/authorsandbooks/authors/fritz/bio.htm.

Fritz, J. 1990. "The Teller and the Tale." In *Worlds of Childhood: The Art and Craft of Writing for Children*, ed. W. Zinsser, 23–46. Boston: Houghton Mifflin.

———. 1992. "Fritz, Jean." In *Major Authors and Illustrators for Children and Young Adults*, eds., Collier L. and J. Nakamura, vol. 2, 884–87. Detroit: Gale Research.

Houghton Mifflin. No date. "Meet the Author: Jean Fritz." Retrieved August 8, 2004, from www.eduplace.com/kids/hmr/mtai.fritz.html.

Kovacs, D., and J. Preller. 1991. *Meet the Authors and Illustrators.* New York: Scholastic.

Scholastic. No date a. Jean Fritz's Biography. Retrieved May 25, 2004, from http://books.scholastic.com/teachers/authorsandbooks/authorstudies/authorhome.

———. No date b. "Jean Fritz's Interview Transcript." Retrieved June 8, 2004, from http://books.scholastic.com/teachers/authorsandbooks/authorstudies/authorhome.jsp?authorID=39&&displayName=Interview%20Transcript.

Jean Fritz Books Used During the Author Study

Fritz, J. 1973. *And Then What Happened, Paul Revere?* New York: G. P. Putnam's Sons.

———. 1973. *And Then What Happened, Paul Revere?* (audio cassette) Norwalk, CT: Western Woods.

———. 1974. *Why Don't You Get a Horse, Sam Adams?* New York: G. P. Putnam's Sons.

———. 1976. *Will You Sign Here, John Hancock?* New York: G. P. Putnam's Sons.

———. 1976. *Can't You Make Them Behave, King George?* New York: G. P. Putnam's Sons.

———. 1982. *Homesick: My Own Story.* New York: G. P. Putnam's Sons.

———. 1985. *China Homecoming.* New York: G. P. Putnam's Sons.

———. 1992a. *George Washington's Mother.* New York: G. P. Putnam's Sons.

———. 1992b. *Surprising Myself.* Katonah, NY: Richard C. Owens.

John predicts, "I think she'll keep repeating the title throughout the book like she did in *Sam Adams*."

Hayley adds, "Jean Fritz will include another Revolutionary War hero in this book like she did in others."

"We will learn whether John Hancock wrote the Declaration of Independence or not," notes Aidan.

After the read-aloud, we confirm or modify our predictions and discuss this larger-than-life patriot.

Jackson notes, "John Hancock was fancy, not sloppy like Sam Adams,"

Melissa adds, "He [Hancock] liked to get all of the attention."

John surmises that Hancock seemed "kind of spoiled but brave."

"He liked to be at parties and in front of the parade," offers Halle.

With each observation, they are asked to substantiate their opinion, which they do with ease, given the alluring details of Hancock's extravagant, attention-seeking, but goodhearted life.

Halle's comment provides the segue to our culminating activity. With the news that Britain had repealed the Stamp Act, John Hancock "threw one of the grandest parties Boston had ever had" (Fritz 1976, 15), a party that spilled out onto the Boston Common. This was one of many parties that Hancock held. How fitting, then, for us to celebrate the end of our author study with a colonial tea party.

After brainstorming ideas for the celebration, we decide that each third grader will choose one of the patriots or patriot's family members whom we have studied. They will dress and act as their character, preparing and rehearsing conversations and speeches they will give during pivotal events of the revolution: the Boston Tea Party, the signing of the Declaration of Independence, Lexington and Concord, Revere's ride, and so on. I stress the importance of rereading their Fritz books so they show mastery of their character and of the historical events through their dialogue.

With the support of parent volunteers, we enjoy a spectacular tea party, drinking raspberry tea (in protest of English teas we were boycotting!) with lumps of sugar and milk, nibbling on hot corn griddle cakes with jam, and toasting "Huzzah!" (a cheer repeated throughout *Will You Sign Here, John Hancock?*) to our colonial heroes. Tables of patriots (male and female) converse over tea about various events. The actors are animated and knowledgeable; many attempt English accents or colonial dialect.

Had I thought of it at the time, I could have made an entrance at the end of the tea party as Jean Fritz, announcing: "I can't believe that all of the patriots whom I've written about are here today." I would introduce myself as Jean Fritz and, one by one, mention the key players and why I enjoyed writing about them. I would then ask if they would like me to read my autobiography, *Surprising Myself* (1992b). Hopefully to "Huzzah, huzzah," I would oblige.

Concluding Thoughts

"Only when a book is written out of passion is there much hope of its being read with passion. Children, above all, need to feel that they are partners in the quest" acknowledges Fritz (1990, 39–40). Instilling a passion about history was one of the primary goals of this author study. I wanted my third graders to understand that the American Revolution was the story of real people who united against an injustice and who dedicated themselves to the creation of a new nation. Fritz's biographies told their stories in a way that captivated my students, in part because of Fritz's efforts to show the interconnectedness of the Founding Fathers—that Sam Adams and John Hancock were good friends, that Paul Revere woke Hancock and Adams in the middle of the night to warn them that the British troops were advancing, and so forth.

A second goal was an introduction to the genre of biography. Sutherland writes: "The three essential ingredients of a good biography are history, the person, and literary artistry. Facts should be authentic and verifiable, the subject should be considered as an individual rather than as a paragon or type; and the writing should be a conscious work of art" (1997, 429). Fritz's works fit the bill—meticulous research and masterful storytelling with a sizeable dash of humor.

And last, but not least, Fritz herself became a focus of study (see Fritz's profile on page 102). Drawing on her engaging autobiographies, *Homesick* (1982) and *China Homecoming* (1985), my third graders first met Fritz as a young girl in China. Identifying with her on many levels, they were hooked. With a few biographies under our belts, we shifted the focus from Fritz the person to Fritz the writer. We examined what she wrote, why she wrote what she wrote, and how she wrote.

In conclusion, this author study, which I have now taught three times, proved to be one of the highlights of each school year. With each enactment, I have never quite been able to put my finger on the variable that ensured its resounding success. Perhaps it is Fritz's love of history that resonates in each and every one of her books. Perhaps it is Fritz's sense of humor that keeps us coming back for more. Perhaps it is the Founding Fathers themselves. Whatever the magic, this author study has been a joy to teach. My third graders not only learned a great deal about American history and the genre of biography but also came to adore a remarkable woman.

6

Spiders and Snakes and Sharks, Oh Yeah!
Outside and Inside Sandra Markle
Special Education, Grades 4 and 5

Karen Centofanti and Carol Brennan Jenkins

As my (Karen) fourth and fifth graders arrive, I ask them to help me attach a poster titled "Who Is Sandra Markle?" to my classroom door (see Figure 6–1). The poster contains a picture of a person dressed in a polar fleece parka, standing in a desolate, snowy wilderness. A scarf covers her face; only dark-tinted goggles are visible.

Mike asks, "I have a question. Is she a penguin explorer?"

"Interesting observation, Mike," I reply. "Over the next two weeks, I'm going to be posting four more posters that feature our mystery person, Sandra Markle. Each poster will reveal a few more clues about her. I want you to be detectives and try to figure out where she is and what she could be doing there. You're going to write your hunches on sticky notes, with your name on the front side and your guess on the back."

After students record a few hunches, I pass out a poetry riddle, explaining: "I also have some clues for you in the form of poetry riddles about different animals. You may not be able to guess what the poetry riddles have to do with Sandra Markle right away, but you will eventually. Here is the first riddle that you'll do for homework. As you read the poem, you'll notice I inserted a line where the animal's name should be. Figure out the name and write it on the line. (Each day, I assign a poetry riddle from either Barbara Esbensen's (1986) collection, *Words with Wrinkled Knees: Animal Poems*, or Byrd Baylor's (1986), *I'm in Charge of Celebrations*.)

Successive posters reveal more clues about Sandra Markle's identity (see Figure 6–1). The pictures, taken from Markle's interactive 1998 website for elementary students (sadly, no longer available), trace her Antarctica expedition to research penguins. The second poster, titled "How Can You Find Out Who Sandra Markle Is?" encourages the students to use the research skills learned earlier in the year. I explain: "I want you to research Sandra Markle. Write your information down on sticky notes, but keep what you learn about Markle a secret."

"Can we use the Internet to look her up?" asks Cody.

FIGURE 6–1 *Sandra Markle bulletin board*

"Good idea, Cody. That's one resource we used in the past to find information. Think about other resources we've consulted. Remember to keep your information about Markle a secret."

When they return after the weekend, we discuss (and post) their research findings:

BRITTANY: I went into AskJeeves.com and I don't think he [Jeeves] likes me. He only told me a little bit about Sandra Markle.

KAREN: What did you learn?

BRITTANY: She's an author about penguins and she writes about kangaroos too.

DELANEY: I found out that she was an elementary science teacher and that her hero is Leanna Landsman.

KAREN: Right. Sandra did teach science and she admires Leanna Landsman, who is president of the magazine *Time for Kids*. Let's add both of your sticky notes to the "What I Know" side of the poster.

I then hang the third poster, which shows Markle photographing penguins. This yields a variety of speculations that range from photographer, to sled-dog racer, to veterinarian of wild animals, to archeologist and poet as well as hunches about where she lives: Alaska, North Pole, and Mount Everest. Their sticky notes are attached to this poster ("What I Know/What I Think I Know About Sandra Markle").

During this second week, they continue to research and post hunches. I congratulate them on their detective work as I post the final poster, which features a close-up photograph of Markle and some basic autobiographical data (see Figure 6–1). I elaborate on some of this data; for example, I explain that Markle loved science as a child because her science teacher's lessons "were always hands-on and for [Sandra], learning science was like discovering how to do magic" (1999, 2). In talking about her writing career, Markle notes, "I can't believe the opportunities writing provides me! I've just returned from spending a month exploring New Zealand, and before that I was in Antarctica for six weeks. I was able to travel to the South Pole—something I've always dreamed of doing—and was transported by helicopter to spend a few hours as the only human in the midst of a penguin rookery" (1988, 135).

My students are curious to know if some of their other hunches, such as whether she is a sled-dog racer, are correct. I tell them that over the course of the author study, we'll continue to research Sandra Markle and post and share their findings.

So begins my fourth and fifth graders' autobiographical encounter with Sandra Markle. With curiosity piqued, our study of Markle's life and literature is launched.

My Classroom

I am a special education teacher who serves children in grades 3, 4, and 5. I provide direct services to small groups of reading-disabled students, implementing the Wilson Reading Program in a pullout model. Committed to the systematic, direct instruction in phonics that characterizes the Wilson program, but intrigued by the potential that a nonfiction author study might have for students who struggle to read, I asked permission to suspend the Wilson program to pursue a study of Sandra Markle and her books. I made the case to my principal and students' parents that success in school is tied to proficiency with nonfiction, "the type of prose that accounts for approximately 80% of the reading and writing experiences students in the United States encounter during their school careers" (Langer 1992, 33). I also noted a recent study of struggling young readers and writers that demonstrated the power of nonfiction literature to usher children into literacy (Caswell and Duke 1998). Given my students' intense interest in animals and in nonfiction in general, I knew that Sandra Markle's books on sharks, snakes, alligators, and bats—creatures of immense intrigue for readers of all ages—would captivate them. I reasoned that if some of my young readers took to Markle's books, and began to read them voluntarily, they might cross that bridge to true literacy. Both my principal and my students' parents gave their consent.

With permission granted, my next challenge was to figure out how to accomplish an author study with students I saw three times a week for about forty minutes each session. I concluded that I would need to solicit the help of the children's parents, and so I wrote a letter asking if they would be willing to help their children with author study assignments. All agreed to support our effort.

Implementing the Sandra Markle Author Study

Having reviewed a number of nonfiction authors, I am intrigued by the photographic splendor of Markle's books. Markle, a former science teacher, has written more than sixty nonfiction books. I settle in to read a sampling of her books to see if they meet the criteria for quality nonfiction literature, as identified by the Massachusetts Curriculum Frameworks. I am impressed with Markle's practice of having experts review her manuscripts for accuracy and currency. I also note her clear, well-organized presentation of content, including her adept handling of technical vocabulary. Her teaching background is evident in the way she consistently ties content to children's experiences and in the way she uses questions to stimulate curiosity and propel the reader. I am not surprised to learn that Markle's works have received many awards.

Knowing my students' affinity for animals, I decide to focus primarily on Markle's popular Outside and Inside series (e.g., *Outside and Inside Alligators* [1998], *Outside and Inside Sharks* [1996], *Outside and Inside Bats* [1997]) and her Growing Up Wild series (e.g., *Growing Up Wild: Bears* [2000], *Growing Up Wild: Penguins* [2002]). In Appendix A, I include a curriculum map that charts the major sequence of events in this author study and the corresponding local and national standards (Massachusetts Curriculum Frameworks and IRA/NCTE Standards for the English Language Arts).

Snake Memories: Personal Response to Outside and Inside Snakes

Posting our poem riddles, I ask my students about their connection to Sandra Markle. Responses range from Cory's "I think Markle wrote these poems," to Delaney's correct guess that "they are the animals in Markle's books." As we review the answers to each animal riddle, I place Markle's corresponding books on a display counter. Their excitement about books such as *Outside and Inside Sharks*, *Outside and Inside Alligators*, and *Outside and Inside Dinosaurs* (2003) is palpable, affirming what surveys of children's reading interests have long indicated about their fascination with animals (Monson and Sebesta 1991). We reread the poetry riddle about rattlesnakes from Byrd Baylor's (1986) collection and then segue to *Outside and Inside Snakes*.

As with each book read in this author study, I first encourage children to share their excitement, fascination, and curiosity about the topic. To model personal response, I read my following snake memories:

> One summer day, I was sitting with my mother on the front cement steps waiting for the ice cream man. Upon seeing the truck, I grabbed a curlicue of the black, wrought-iron railing but felt something move. A long, black snake suddenly unwound itself from the curlicue and darted off. I screamed and thought my heart was going to pound its way right out of my chest! The worst part was watching it slither underneath the cement steps. Every time I walked out my front door, I worried about that snake attacking me.
>
> The following spring, I happened to notice a baby toad hopping toward the hole under our cement steps. I loved toads and frogs; I used to catch them with my friends and then turn them loose. I knew that the baby toad was a goner if I didn't act fast so

I reached down to pluck it up. But the snake's head darted out, bit my hand, and then swallowed the toad whole! I was horrified and ran into the house. My mother inspected the bite that itched like crazy and assured me that I was okay. To this day, I still cringe when I see a snake but am working on conquering my fears.

The students gasp, laugh, ask questions, relate sympathy, and begin to talk about similar experiences. I then ask them to write their snake experiences as a homework assignment.

I hold up *Outside and Inside Snakes* and comment that based on their personal responses, they seem to know a good deal about snakes. I revisit the idea that good readers tap their background knowledge before and during the process of reading a nonfiction book and then I pass out an anticipation guide. We chorally read each item and discuss possible answers, and then they individually complete their guide. Delaney's completed guide is presented in Figure 6–2. I explain that I will read *Outside and Inside Snakes* over the next two days and that they will have a chance to verify and expand their knowledge about snakes.

Personal Responses and Prior Knowledge

We begin our next session with their snake experiences. Delaney volunteers to read her response:

> When I was eight years old I was at Petco . . . with my mom, my friend, Meg, and her mom. They have all kinds of animals and animal supplies at Petco. A young man with a snake asked if Meg and I wanted to hold it, and we said yes. Luckily our mothers were shopping somewhere else in the store. They would never have let us do this! The snake's name was Slithers because he liked to wander off. I think it was python, but I wasn't sure. It was very long, almost longer than me! He was all green. Slithers was very wiggly. He was so wiggly he almost got away! Meg sort of liked holding the snake, but I loved it! It was fun!

Questions and answers follow, along with tales of holding snakes at birthday parties and zoos. Danny then reads his content-rich piece (see Figure 6–3). I note that Danny is so knowledgeable about snakes that he could have contributed some items, such as what snakes eat, to our anticipation guide.

With *Outside and Inside Snakes* in hand, we discuss the features that make it a quality nonfiction book: excellent photographs, current publication date, consultation with experts, glossary, and so on. We talk about why Markle asked snake experts to review her manuscript (after all, she was a science teacher). We discuss the difference between a science writer and herpetologist, and why it is important for Markle to verify that her information is accurate and up-to-date.

We then review our range of answers to our anticipation guide and settle in to enjoy *Outside and Inside Snakes*. We agree that as answers to our anticipation guide items occur, we will stop to confirm or reject, recording correct information when appropriate. As I read, my fourth and fifth graders are completely absorbed. They love the pictures, interject comments, listen intently, and ask questions. In addition, they

Name _Delaney_   Date _____

Outside and Inside Snakes by Sandra Markle
Extended Anticipatory Guide

Directions: Read each statement. Mark each statement as True or False by placing a check mark in the appropriate column.

True	False	
✓		1. Snakes can eat things larger than their heads.
✓		2. Snakes do not blink.
	✓	3. If you touch a snake it will feel warm and slimy.
✓		4. Snakes shed their skin once every 3 years.
✓		5. Snakes can smell with their tongues.
	✓	6. All snakes are hunters.
✓		7. All snakes swallow their food whole.
	✓	8. All snakes inject a poison called venom when they eat.
✓		9. Snakes can live 3 weeks without food.
✓		10. All snakes hatch from eggs.

PART TWO

Directions: If the information you read about in this book supports your answer above, place a check mark in the "I was right!" column. If you were wrong, put a check mark in that column and answer in your own words "Here's what I found out."

I was right!	I was wrong.	Here's what I found out.
1. ✓		
2. ✓		
3. ✓		
4.	✓	They shed 3-7 X a year
5. ✓		
6.	✓	all snakes are hunters
7. ✓		
8. ✓		
9. ✓		
10.	✓	Some are born live

FIGURE 6–2 *Delaney's anticipation guide*

remain on alert for the answers in our anticipation guide. When they add up their scores, all but one get five or more items correct.

Students Construct Their Own Anticipation Guides

Before I even finish reading *Outside and Inside Snakes*, Aaron pleads, "Can we read Markle's alligator book next, please?" Others chime in with their requests. This sets

Name Danny

Date

Aesthetic Response to "Outside and Inside Snakes"

Directions: Choose a or b below to write about. Don't forget you need a topic sentence, details, and a closing sentence.

a.)   Tell about a time you saw a snake. Where were you? What happened? What did you do? What did the snake do? How did you feel?

b.)   Do you like snakes? Why or why not? Explain how you were influenced to feel the way you do.

I like Snakes because to feel them they are smooth and silky. They sliver on the ground so gracefully. Another reason I like garden snakes because they do not bite people they help us by eating insects, especially mosquitoes. Snakes do not bother you, they are more afraid of you than we are of them. I began to like snakes when I caught a garden snake in the yard and I could examine how the snake was so harmless and so scared of me and tried to get away so quickly from me. Snakes can be found any where, under porches, in the grass, or woods. They can even get into your house. The funniest thing about snakes is when your mowing the lawn and you can see them scurry around so they don't get caught in the blades.

FIGURE 6–3   *Danny's snake memory*

the stage for having each student take on the role of budding expert. I remark that each will choose and read one Outside and Inside book and create an anticipation guide for peers to complete. I explain that they will need to identify the key information about the topic, write true statements that are accurate and false statements that appear plausible, as well as revise and edit their statements for clarity, accuracy and mechanics. They love the idea of designing their own guides.

To ensure success, I walk them through the process I used to create my anticipation guide on snakes, using overheads of sections from Markle's snake book to illustrate decisions I made. These guidelines are summarized in Figure 6–4.

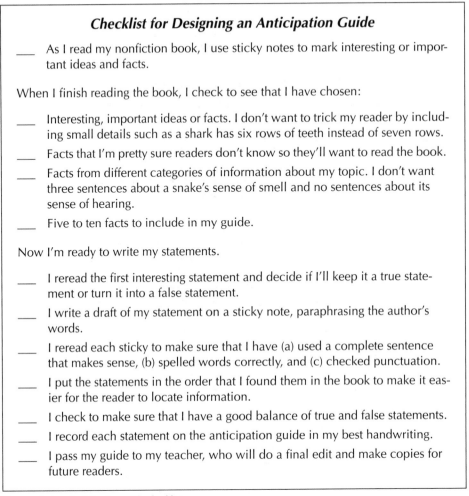

Checklist for Designing an Anticipation Guide

____ As I read my nonfiction book, I use sticky notes to mark interesting or important ideas and facts.

When I finish reading the book, I check to see that I have chosen:

____ Interesting, important ideas or facts. I don't want to trick my reader by including small details such as a shark has six rows of teeth instead of seven rows.

____ Facts that I'm pretty sure readers don't know so they'll want to read the book.

____ Facts from different categories of information about my topic. I don't want three sentences about a snake's sense of smell and no sentences about its sense of hearing.

____ Five to ten facts to include in my guide.

Now I'm ready to write my statements.

____ I reread the first interesting statement and decide if I'll keep it a true statement or turn it into a false statement.

____ I write a draft of my statement on a sticky note, paraphrasing the author's words.

____ I reread each sticky to make sure that I have (a) used a complete sentence that makes sense, (b) spelled words correctly, and (c) checked punctuation.

____ I put the statements in the order that I found them in the book to make it easier for the reader to locate information.

____ I check to make sure that I have a good balance of true and false statements.

____ I record each statement on the anticipation guide in my best handwriting.

____ I pass my guide to my teacher, who will do a final edit and make copies for future readers.

FIGURE 6–4   *Anticipation guide checklist*

Most students do a fine job on this assignment, as Arianna's guide in Figure 6–5 shows. I am pleased that many create items that are culled from across their book (and not just from the first few pages), that center on the interesting facts about their animal, and that effectively manipulate the veracity of the statement. As anticipated, some need support rereading and comprehending their text, selecting the most relevant information, and transforming statements into plausible false items.

If I taught this unit again, I would read a second Markle book and create an anticipation guide step-by-step with the group before having the students attempt their own. Prior to reading this book, I would do a KWL to establish common knowledge about the animal and discuss why it is more effective to not include this general information on an anticipation guide. After reading the book, I would note that Markle does not use headings and ask them to suggest headings for various sections, writing their contributions on sticky notes and adhering them to the book. I would then show them how to design items that span this range of content and represent major ideas. I also would suggest that they write each statement on a separate sticky note so that they could arrange the items in the order of the book as well as revise and edit at a later point.

That said, in my estimation, this activity was the highlight of the author study, generating the most excitement. Some were so taken with this idea that they independently created multiple anticipation guides. Cody, for example, designed four guides for Markle's books on bats, alligators, sharks, and dinosaurs; Arianna wrote three guides for bats, rats, and kangaroos. Central to the success of this activity was the invitation to exchange their guides with each other (see Brittany's responses in part two to Arianna's anticipation guide on kangaroos in Figure 6–5). They were willing to invest the time because others would use the guides—writing and reading for a genuine purpose. I placed multiple copies of their guides as well as the corresponding books in a special display to celebrate the guide writers and to entice prospective readers.

Name Arianna Date

Anticipatory Guide for Kangaroos (Outside and Inside)

Directions: Read and mark each statement as True or False by placing a check mark in the appropriate column.

True	False	
		1. Kangaroos hop on two feet.
		2. They do not use their tails for support.
		3. Kangaroos live in Australia and New Zealand.
		4. They have 7 teeth.
		5. They can get to five feet tall.
		*6. A baby Kangaroo is called a Joey.
		*7. They have a strong Tendon in their legs.

*extra credit

PART TWO - Completed by Brittany

Directions: If the information you read about in this book supports your answer above, place a check mark in the "I was right!" column. If you were wrong, put a check mark in that column and answer in your own words "Here's what I found out."

I was right!	I was wrong.	Here's what I found out.
1. ✓		1
2.	✓	2 It helps the Kangaroo Balance while hopping
3. ✓		3
4. ✓		4
5.	✓	5 Red Kangaroos can be as tall as the tallest basketball player
*6.	✓	6 A baby Kangaroo is called a Joey
*7. ✓		7

FIGURE 6–5 *Brittany's response to Arianna's guide*

How Does Markle Organize Her Information? Analyzing Text Structures

Convinced that my students' comprehension and composition will be significantly enhanced with knowledge about the way nonfiction authors organize their information, I first tap their understanding of story structure and then use it to segue to nonfiction text structure. I place a story map on the overhead and ask its purpose. Because they have completed story maps for picture books and chapter books, they target the story grammar elements (e.g., setting, characters, problem, attempts/outcomes, and resolution). We review the importance of using this framework when we are both reading and writing stories. I hold up *Outside and Inside Snakes* and ask if I can use the story map to show how this book is organized. I ask if there were any characters in this book who had problems that needed to be solved. They decide that a story map won't work because Markle's book contains facts about snakes, not a story about a snake's adventure. I elaborate on their response, pointing out that if Markle's book were called "The Day Jimmy's Boa Ate the Wash," we'd probably be able to use a story map.

I explain that nonfiction authors organize their information differently from fiction authors, and that, instead of one map, there is a map for each different text structure. I note that Sandra Markle uses at least four text structures in different sections of *Outside and Inside Snakes*. To illustrate the compare-and-contrast structure, I place a blank Venn diagram on the overhead and ask if it looks familiar. They note that they've used it to compare characters and plots in stories. I concur and remark that nonfiction writers also use Venn diagrams to organize their information. We chorally read the following page from *Outside and Inside Snakes*:

> So what's underneath a snake's skin? Bones, for one thing.
>
> A building has a strong framework to support it and give it shape. A snake's body, like yours, has a framework—a bony skeleton. But a snake's skeleton is very different from yours. For one thing, you have arms and legs. A snake does not. You also have only thirty-three backbones and twenty-four ribs. A long snake may have more than three hundred backbones, or vertebrae, with a pair of ribs attached to all backbones but those of the neck and tail.
>
> Do you wonder why a snake's skeleton has so many backbones? Its body, like yours, can only bend where two bones meet. Having lots of small bones lets it coil and bend easily. (1995, 15)

Then, I ask what Markle is comparing and record their responses—the snake's skeleton on one side of the Venn and the human skeleton on the other. I reiterate that these two outer circles allow us to contrast the two types of skeletons. I then ask what label I should use to describe the middle oval.

JESSE: How about "Both," for how they are the same.
KAREN: Good. Reread the first sentence in Markle's page and tell me something I can write.

CODY: They both have skeletons.

KAREN: Good! [*I write "have skeletons" in the oval.*] Note the key word, *like*, in this sentence: "A snake's body, like yours, has a framework, or skeleton." That key word, *like*, lets you know that the author is comparing two things. . . . Can you imagine what we'd look like if we didn't have bones? We'd just be a puddle of muscles and skin on the floor! [*laughter*]

KAREN: Let's read the next sentence: "But a snake's skeleton is very different from yours." There's another key word, *different*. What should I write and where should I put it?

Upon completion of this Venn diagram, I explain that Markle uses this compare-and-contrast text structure to organize particular content in all of her Outside and Inside books. For example, I read a passage that compares human and shark teeth in *Outside and Inside Sharks* (1996) and ask what is being compared and why. We discuss potency of comparison to link the familiar with the unfamiliar and to evoke strong images that help us grasp and recall difficult concepts. I then ask them to take out the Markle book that they chose to read to create their anticipation guide, and to find a compare-and-contrast passage.

KAREN: What key words are you going to look for?

CODY: *Like* and *unlike*.

DANYA: *Same* and *different*.

KAREN: Good. A section on bones is a good start because Markle almost always compares our skeleton to that of the animal she's writing about. Jesse, did you find one?

JESSE: Yes, she compares fish with sharks.

KAREN: Let's put a sticky note there so you can find that again.

Other students share their discoveries and mark them with sticky notes. For homework, they fill out a Venn diagram to show the comparison. The next day we review why Markle organizes her information this way and how Venn diagrams facilitate both comprehension and composition.

Over the next few sessions, I introduce two additional text structures: sequence and description. As with the compare-and-contrast lessons, I begin with a passage from *Outside and Inside Snakes* and have them help me complete a graphic organizer. For example, to illustrate sequence, I select a passage on the snake's digestive system. Using a numbered chart, we paraphrase each step of a snake's digestion, paying attention to signal words (e.g., *first, second, next, then, finally*). We repeat with a passage on the molting process. For homework, students are assigned to search their Markle book to find a sequence passage and complete the graphic organizer. After we have examined the description text structure in the same fashion, I review the three text structures by playing tick-tack-toe with passages from *Outside and Inside Snakes* and asking teams to identify the structure.

I then ask the students to think about the overall organizational structure of *Outside and Inside Snakes* in order to figure out the primary text structure of this book. I ask, "Did Markle organize it as a sequence book, using the whole book to explain the snake's life cycle? Or did she decide to organize the whole book by comparing and contrasting snakes and humans? Or did Markle mainly describe everything a reader would want to know about snakes, therefore using mostly description text structures along with a few sequence passages and a few compare-and-contrast passages interspersed?" After much discussion and a rough count of the types of structures used throughout *Outside and Inside Snakes,* we conclude that this book, like all of the Outside and Inside books, is primarily description.

To further illustrate primary text structure, I show *Growing Up Wild: Bears* (2000) and ask them to think about the title in order to figure out what organizational scheme Markle used when writing this book. They choose sequence; I do a quick picture walk to confirm. I then show Markle's *After the Spill: The* Exxon Valdez *Disaster, Then and Now* (1999), the book that we will be talking about in our next lesson. Some guess compare-and-contrast and others guess sequence, noting the *Then and Now* tag. I comment that they'll find out if they're correct during the next session.

Book Talks: Sustaining Interest in Sandra Markle

With the goal of having my students share their excitement about Markle's books with their general education peers, I model a book talk using *After the Spill: The* Exxon Valdez *Disaster, Then and Now.* I begin by reading the book title, showing a photograph of an oil-soaked bird, and asking what they think happened.

CODY: An oil spill.

KAREN: Yes, this bird was caught in one of the worst oil spills that ever happened. In 1989, this ship [*showing picture of the* Exxon Valdez] was leaving Prince William Sound in Alaska when the captain suddenly noticed jagged boulders ahead. He tried to turn the ship, but it was too late.

CODY: This is sort of like the *Titanic.*

KAREN: Yes, in that rocks tore an enormous hole in the hull, except the ship didn't sink and people didn't die. What do you think happened to the oil?

JESSE: It drained out.

KAREN. Yes, can you imagine what millions of gallons of this black, crude oil—enough to fill fourteen Olympic swimming pools—did to the environment?

BRITTANY: It ruined everything.

KAREN: At first, the experts thought that the oil would stay pooled around the ship. But something unexpected happened. Can you guess?

CODY: Someone lit a match.

KAREN: No, but that would be awful, wouldn't it? Something else happened that made the spill much worse.

ARIANNA: The animals swam in it.

KAREN: Yes, that happened, but actually a fierce storm with high winds hit the area and spread the oil onto the shores. [*Reads a caption about a bird covered in oil.*] Who knows how birds clean themselves?

DELANEY: They use their beaks.

KAREN: Yes, they pull their feathers through their beaks; it's called preening. That's what these birds did. What do you think happened?

CODY: They got oil in their mouths.

KAREN: Yes, many birds were poisoned by the toxic oil and died. Many also died from the cleaning that the volunteers tried to give; it was too stressful to be cleaned gently with a toothbrush.

And so the book talk continues. My students are intrigued. I end with a picture of an oil-saturated sea otter and tell them they can read the book to find out what happened to it as well as to the people who lived in the area. I ask whether my book talk has made them want to read the book. All answer affirmatively. I ask what they think makes a good book talk. They note that it's a good idea to show some photographs to get listeners interested. They also mention that you have to "really know" the book so you can answer questions and that you should like the book, so that you can be convincing when talking about it.

Complimenting their ideas, I then explain that they will have a chance to persuade others to read one of their favorite Markle books. I share how I planned my book talk on *After the Spill* during our next session (see Figure 6–6). Working in pairs of two, students then brainstorm ideas for their book talk. I confer with partners, responding to their ideas, referring them to the book talk guidelines (Figure 6–6), and encouraging them to rehearse. I tell them I am so excited about their book talks that I'm going to videotape them. My original plan is to videotape their book talks so that if they choose, they can show the videotape in their general education classrooms to hook their peers on Markle's books. However, with the exception of Mike (see Figure 6–7), most are so shy while conducting their book talks in front of their small group of peers that I decide not to mention this option. Shyness notwithstanding, many do a good job at implementing their book talks.

As Figure 6–7 and the following excerpts from Mike's book talk reveal, he steals the show. To prepare, he places a stuffed penguin, a magazine cover, and Markle's penguin book on a chair. He then walks from the sidelines, wearing a paper hat (simulating Markle's polar hat on the book jacket), singing, "Dun, dun, dun, da, dun, dun, dun da . . . ," and announcing, *The Sandra Markle Show*. In a high-pitched voice, he begins:

Hello, everybody, my name is Sandra Markle and I made this book, especially for Mike [*big smile*]. He loves this book. OK, the title is *Growing Up Wild: Penguins*. This is an Adelie penguin [*pointing to a photo*]. See how very cute they are. . . . Let's turn the page. This Adelie penguin is calling his new girlfriend over to mate with him. And this is when the egg comes out of the Adelie penguin. This is when the male penguin, or father penguin, is keeping the chick warm. And [on] this page right here is the Adelie penguin building its nest. Isn't that amazing how they would pick up

---

Book Talk Ideas*

- Dress up as the author or topic focus.
- Bring a prop that ties to book's topic (such as a hat, a stuffed animal, a puppet, a toy, a picture, a map, or a feather) to use at some point during the book talk.
- Show the book's cover and read the title. Tell the main idea of the book—what it is about.
- Share a personal experience you've had that relates to the topic.
- Tell your audience how much you enjoyed the book and why.
- Show an interesting picture and ask a question that makes the audience think about the picture; repeat with a few more pictures. Have these pages marked with sticky notes for easy access.
- Read an interesting excerpt from the book and ask a prediction question to keep your audience involved.
- Leave your audience curious about and excited to read the book.

  Remember to speak and read clearly and loudly enough to be heard.
  Make eye contact.
  Be expressive and show your enthusiasm.

* Use some, but not all of these ideas. Use your own ideas too.

FIGURE 6–6   *Book talk guidelines*

those pebbles and walk over to the nest? Now this right here [*pointing to a photo of baby chick's beak in its mother's mouth*], don't think it's [the mother] eating this penguin [baby]. No, get that thought out of your head. It's trying to feed the penguin. See, see how it [the baby] picks out the food it wants. . . . [*Mike continues to narrate in this manner, pointing to various photographs throughout the book.*] What do you think this penguin [a single penguin perched on an icy ledge with wings spread] is doing—(a) feeding, (b) mating, (c) nesting, or (d) diving? [*Peers begin to answer.*] Well, you have to read this book to find out.

Closing the book, Mike announces, "And now I have a special guest on my show. Dun, dun, dun, da. *The Sandra Markle Talk Show.* This is a King penguin [*holding the stuffed penguin*]. If you want to hear some things about this penguin, he talks and you have to listen to it."

Mike then waddles up to the camera and presses the stuffed penguin's recording button. The audience learns what the King penguin eats and the sound it makes. Mike then waddles around, calling, "Aaaah, aaaah, aaaah." Next, he shows the cover of a *National Geographic* magazine and says, "Now these are King penguins with their chick.

FIGURE 6–7   *Mike gives his book talk*

This is the most famous picture of penguins on a magazine. OK, I'm going to pick someone out of the audience to come up here and make the penguin sounds like this, 'Aaaah, aaaah.'"

Danny volunteers first, followed by Brittany. Mike then ends the show: "I guess I'll see you next time on *The Sandra Markle Show.*"

As you scan the suggested ideas in Figure 6–6, you can see that Mike experimented with many of these guidelines as well as integrated his own ideas, appropriated probably from talk shows on television. He planned his show independently, wanting it to be a surprise for everyone in his audience, including me. He certainly succeeded!

In hindsight, it would have been productive to have Mike do his book talk a few days before the others so that they would have had exposure to a second book talk and an opportunity to compare Mike's book talk against the guidelines, sharing what they liked about it. Mike also could have viewed the tape and explained changes that he might make. I then would try to find the time to have each student do a dry run in front of a small group of third graders, receive feedback, and then revise and perform for peers.

A Visit with "Sandra Markle": Biographical Response

Hunches about Markle as a person and as a writer continue to be posted on the Markle bulletin board. For example, nearly all write that Markle loves animals, that she must feel sad when an animal dies, that she must be rich to be able to fly everywhere to photograph different kinds of animals, and that she loves to write because she has authored so many books.

At the end of the author study, my assistant, Geri, who has auburn hair like Markle, agrees to become Sandra Markle. On a snowy day, I ask the fourth and fifth graders to put on their coats and hats because we are going outside. Bundled in a snow parka, Geri darts out from a side door, greets the children, and tells them that she is "Sandra Markle," and that she has stopped by to thank them for reading her books. She tells them that she'd be happy to answer any questions they have. The class laughs and plays along. For example, the students want to know how cold it was in Antarctica when she was filming the penguins, if she was afraid when photographing the bears, whether she has any children and if they travel with her, and what made her want to be a writer. "Sandra" does a fine job fielding many of their questions, having absorbed the autobiographical content that I prepared for her (see the author profile on the next page).

This event leads to a discussion about how we might let the real Sandra Markle know how much we have enjoyed her books. We decide to write a biopoem about Sandra Markle. At the beginning of the school year, students created biopoems as a way of introducing themselves. Familiar with the poem's format, they work individually to pen what they know about Markle. I place a blank biopoem on the overhead, and we take turns sharing responses, which I record, tallying repeat responses. Because there are tie votes for many attributes, we weigh their ideas in order to choose the best. Our final draft reads as follows:

Sandra
Four words that describe her: animal lover, intelligent, photographer, writer
Daughter of Robert and Dorothy
Who feels excited, brave, caring
Who needs new ideas, good pictures, money to travel
Who gives information, books, happiness
Who fears people not liking her books, animals being hurt, running out of money
Who would like to see clean and safe habitats for animals, free animals, new books
Resident of New Zealand
Markle

Sandra Markle

Born: October 11, 1946, in Fostoria, Ohio

Careers: teacher, photographer, author

Awards: More than thirty from organizations such as International Reading Association, Children's Book Council, and Science Teacher Association

Home: Amberely, New Zealand

A former elementary school teacher, an award-winning author of more than eighty children's books, and a nationally recognized consultant in science education, Sandra Markle brings complex and fascinating scientific ideas and discoveries within the cognitive grasp of elementary school children. During her first year of teaching, most of her students were children of migrant farmers in a small Ohio town. Believing that children learn science best by doing, she developed lessons that tapped their interests and involved them in hands-on learning experiences. Subsequently, she taught elementary science for eleven years but continued to be disappointed with the quality of nonfiction literature for children. Recognizing this need, Markle decided to become a full-time writer. Grounded in her training and classroom experience in science education, she transmits her passion for science to elementary students through children's books and, most recently, through the development of Kit and Kaboodle, an Internet-based learning environment.

Markle on Markle: Quotes About Her Childhood

On her favorite food: "Chocolate" (Christchurch City Libraries n.d.).

On her most loved book: "I still love *A Wrinkle in Time* by Madeline L'Engle" (Christchurch City Libraries n.d.).

On who inspired her: "I adored my grandfather and was his shadow. His love of the outdoors, natural curiosity, and creative spirit still inspire me" (Christchurch City Libraries n.d.).

On her favorite subject: "The journey that led to my writing science books for children started when I was in the fifth grade. That was about the time Sputnik made everyone decide kids should learn about science but before anyone had yet published an official science textbook. So my first experience with science was when my hometown's (Fostoria, Ohio) one and only science teacher arrived twice a month to guide my class through hands-on experiments or take us outdoors to explore the world for ourselves. As far as I was concerned, science was magical, amazing, and fun. I was hooked!" (Charlesbridge n.d.).

On what she was like as a student: "Hard working, curious, enjoyed teamwork and individual challenges" (Christchurch City Libraries n.d.).

On writing: "I always enjoyed writing and illustrating. . . . I was forever making my own books on sheets of folded paper" (Upper Arlington School District 2003).

Markle on Markle: Quotes About Her Writing Process

On why she loves writing: "Writing nonfiction science has given me an excuse to get to know many fascinating people and has taken me to amazing places—even to the end of the earth. For example, while working on *Growing Up Wild: Penguins* (Atheneum/Simon and Schuster), I went to Antarctica and spent a summer living with 60,000 Adelie penguins while they were raising their chicks. . . . *Growing Up Wild: Bears* (Atheneum/Simon and Schuster) took me to Denali National Park in Alaska to see bears up-close. I got so close to my subject for *Outside and Inside: Snakes* (Atheneum/Simon & Schuster) that I was bitten on the forehead by a large boa constrictor. Luckily, they're non-poisonous so my adventures are still continuing" (Charlesbridge n.d.).

On other hair-raising experiences while in Antarctica: "I will never forget being on my knees photographing penguins just an arm's length from the open sea when a killer whale stuck its head up and looked me in the eye. I will also never forget huddling in my sleeping bag while my only shelter, a tent, was ripped apart by hurricane force winds. From these experiences came four books. . . . My trips to Antarctica also led to my producing one of the first-ever interactive websites about my experiences" (Charlesbridge n.d.).

On a special place to write: "Anywhere I am—once on a beach in Fiji and once in a tent in Antarctica" (Christchurch City Libraries n.d.).

On advice for budding authors: "WRITE!! But also, periodically, read what you're writing out loud and listen with a reader's ear. Always remember, writing began as a way to record what people were saying. It's still that" (Christchurch City Libraries n.d.).

Biographical References

Charlesbridge. No date. "Sandra Markle." Retrieved February 8, 2006, from www.charlesbridge.com/msp/catalog/contributor/detail.do?id=10704.

Christchurch City Libraries. No date. "Interviews with NZ Childrens Authors." Retrieved February 8, 2006, from www.library.christchurch.org.nz/Kids/Childrens-Authors/SandraMarkle.asp.

Markle, S. 1988. "Sandra Markle." In *Something About the Author: Autobiography Series*, ed. A. Sarkissian, 132–37. Detroit: Gale Research.

———. 2005a. "Author's Note." Retrieved February 7, 2005, from www.charles-bridge.com/msp/catalog/product/detail.do?id+11211.

———. 2005b. *A Mother's Journey.* Watertown, MA: Charlesbridge.

Upper Arlington School District. "Sandra Markle." Retrieved February 5, 2006, from school.uaschools.org/greensview/ohioauthors/markle,sandra.htm.

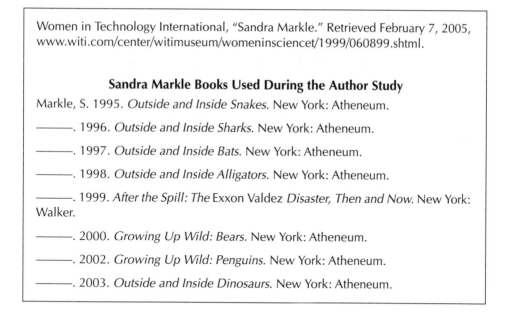

Women in Technology International, "Sandra Markle." Retrieved February 7, 2005, www.witi.com/center/witimuseum/womeninsciencet/1999/060899.shtml.

Sandra Markle Books Used During the Author Study

Markle, S. 1995. *Outside and Inside Snakes.* New York: Atheneum.

———. 1996. *Outside and Inside Sharks.* New York: Atheneum.

———. 1997. *Outside and Inside Bats.* New York: Atheneum.

———. 1998. *Outside and Inside Alligators.* New York: Atheneum.

———. 1999. *After the Spill: The* Exxon Valdez *Disaster, Then and Now.* New York: Walker.

———. 2000. *Growing Up Wild: Bears.* New York: Atheneum.

———. 2002. *Growing Up Wild: Penguins.* New York: Atheneum.

———. 2003. *Outside and Inside Dinosaurs.* New York: Atheneum.

I tell them that I'll send our poem to Markle's publisher, but not to be disappointed if we don't receive a reply. I explain that authors receive many letters and often don't have the time to reply because they are so busy writing their books. In a final tribute to Sandra Markle, we hang our biopoem on the door of our classroom so that other students in our school who initially inspected the posters about this incognito person can learn more about her.

Concluding Comments

Long after the author study ended, my fourth and fifth graders continued to ask for Sandra Markle read-alouds and were delighted when I added other Markle books to our class library. A few signed out Markle's books from the school library on a regular basis and brought them to class to show me what they were reading. Simply put, they were taken with this author and her curiosity about and love for animals.

As noted earlier in this chapter, my primary responsibility as a special needs teacher is to advance the decoding skills of my students by implementing the Wilson reading system. I took on the challenge of introducing this Sandra Markle study because I know that while decoding skills are essential, they are not enough to ensure that my students become lifelong readers. I decided to suspend the Wilson program for the month of January, a low-energy time of the year, to see if Markle would engage them. What I thought would be a four-week unit extended to a six-week unit, in part because of their excitement about the author study, and in part because of the extra time needed to fully implement lessons. In addition, parental support with homework assignments ranged from excellent to nonexistent, requiring additional in-class time. All in all, though, the Sandra Markle author study proved to be a worthy addition to my literacy program. It gave my students multiple opportunities to apply their decoding skills in context. It introduced them to the ways in which one author organizes her content, furthering their comprehension in the process. In addition, it sparked a genuine interest in nonfiction literature and in the person who crafted these works.

References

Amazing Animals of the World. 1995. 24 Vols. Danbury, CT: Grolier Education Corp.

Au, K. 1998. "Social Constructivism and the School Literacy Learning Needs of Students of Diverse Backgrounds." *Journal of Literacy Research* 30(2): 297–319.

Avi. 1991. Author's Commentary. In *Children's Literature Review,* ed. G. Selnick and S. Gunton, 1–15. Detroit: Gale Research.

Bakhtin, M. 1986. *Speech Genres and Other Late Essays.* Austin: University of Texas Press.

Bamford R., and J. Kristo. 1998. *Making Facts Come Alive: Choosing Quality Nonfiction Literature K–8.* Norwood, MA: Christopher Gordon.

Bear, D., S. Templeton, L. Helman, and T. Baren. 2003. "Orthographic Development and Learning to Read in Different Languages." In *English Learners: Reaching the Highest Level of English Literacy,* ed. G. Garcia, 71–95. Newark, DE: International Reading Association.

Bender, D., B. Leone, S. Barbour, B. Szumski, and E. Morey. 1998. *Readings on "The Scarlet Letter."* San Diego: Greenhaven.

Buss, K., and L. Karnowski. 2002. *Reading and Writing Nonfiction Genres.* Newark, DE: International Reading Association.

Caswell, L. J., and N. K. Duke. 1998. "Nonnarrative as a Catalyst for Literacy Development." *Language Arts* 75(2): 108–17.

Children's Literature Review. Detroit MI: Gale Research Co.

Cole, J. 1996. *On the Bus with Joanna Cole: A Creative Autobiography.* Portsmouth, NH: Heinemann.

Collier, L. and J. Nakamura. 1992. *Major Authors and Illustrators for Children and Young Adults.* Detroit: Gale Research.

Consuelo, Sr. M. 1967. "What Do First Graders Like to Read?" *Catholic School Journal* 67: 42–43.

Coppola, J., C. Dawson, J. George, and D. MacLean. 2005. "In My Country, We Don't Write Stories, We Tell Our Stories": Writing with English-Language Learners in the Primary Grades. In *Learning to Write, Writing to Learn: Theory and Research in Practice,* ed. R. Indrisano and J. Paratore, 40–56. Newark, DE: International Reading Association.

Cullinan, B. and L. Galda. 1994. *Literature and the Child.* New York: Harcourt Brace.

Duke, N., and S. Bennett-Armistead. 2003. *Reading and Writing Informational Text in the Primary Grades.* New York: Scholastic.

Duke, N., and J. Kays. 1998. "'Can I Say "Once Upon a Time"?' Kindergarten Children Developing Knowledge of Information Book Language." *Early Childhood Research Quarterly* 13: 295–318.

Duthie, C. 1996. *True Stories: Nonfiction in the Primary Classroom.* Portland, ME: Stenhouse.

Englert, C., and E. Hiebert. 1984. "Children's Developing Awareness of Text Structure in Expository Materials." *Journal of Educational Psychology* 76: 65–74.

Fitzgerald, J., and G. Noblitt. 1999. "About Hopes, Aspirations, and Uncertainties: First Grade English-Language Learners' Emergent Reading." *Journal of Literacy Research* 31(2): 133–82.

Fountas, I., and G. S. Pinnell. 1996. *Guided Reading: Good First Teaching for All.* Portsmouth, NH: Heinemann.

———. 2001. *Guiding Readers and Writers: Grades 3–6.* Portsmouth, NH: Heinemann.

Freedman, R. 1992. "Fact or Fiction." In *Using Nonfiction Trade Books in the Elementary Classroom: From Ants to Zeppelins*, eds. E. Freeman and D. Person. Urbana, IL: NCTE.

Fritz, J. 1982. *Homesick: My Own Story.* New York: Putnam.

Frye, N. 1963. *The Well-Tempered Critic.* Bloomington: Indiana University Press.

Garcia, E. 2005. *Teaching and Learning in Two Languages: Bilingualism and Schooling in the United States.* New York: Teachers College Press.

Gardner, H. 1993. *Multiple Intelligences: The Theory in Practice.* New York: Basic Books.

Gay, P. 2004. "The Most Surprising Book I Read." In *Remarkable Reads: 34 Writers and Their Adventures in Reading*, ed. J. P. Zane. New York: W. W. Norton.

Gersten, R., and R. Jimenez. 1998. *Promoting Learning for Culturally and Linguistically Diverse Students.* Belmont, CA: Wadsworth.

Golden, J. 1984. "Children's Concept of Story in Reading and Writing." *The Reading Teacher* 37: 578–85.

Harvey, S. 1998. *Nonfiction Matters: Reading, Writing, and Research in Grades 3–8.* Portland, ME: Stenhouse.

———. 2000. *Strategies That Work: Teaching Comprehension to Enhance Understanding.* Portland, ME: Stenhouse.

Hawthorne, N. 1850/1967. *The Scarlet Letter.* New York: Lancer.

Huck, C., S. Hepler, and J. Hickman. 1987. *Children's Literature in the Elementary School.* New York: Holt, Rinehart and Winston.

International Reading Association and National Council of Teachers of English. 1996. *Standards for the English Language Arts.* Newark, DE: International Reading Association. Urbana, IL: National Council of Teachers of English.

Ivey, G., and K. Broaddus. 2001. "'Just Plain Reading': A Survey of What Makes Students Want to Read in Middle School Classrooms." *Reading Research Quarterly* 36(4): 350–77.

Jacobs, H. H. 1997. *Mapping the Big Picture: Integrating Curriculum and Assessment K–12.* Alexandria, VA: Association for Supervision and Curriculum Development.

Jenkins, C. B. 1999. *The Allure of Authors: Author Studies in the Elementary Classroom.* Portsmouth, NH: Heinemann.

———. 2006. "'Did I Tell You That You Are the BEST Writer in the World?': Author Studies in the Elementary Classroom." *Journal of Children's Literature.* 32(1): 64–78.

Jenkins, C. B., and A. Earle. 2006. *Once Upon a Fact: Helping Children Write Nonfiction.* New York: Teachers College Press.

Kamberelis, G., and T. Bovino. 1999. "Cultural Artifacts as Scaffolds for Genre Development." *Reading Research Quarterly* 34(2): 138–70.

Keck, J. 1992. "Using a Nonfiction Author Study in the Classroom." In *Using Nonfiction Trade Books in the Elementary Classroom: From Ants to Zeppelins,* ed. E. Freeman and D. Person. 123–130. Urbana, IL: National Council of Teacher of English.

Kidspiration. 2004. Portland, OR: Inspirational Softwear, Inc.

Kirsch, D. 1975. "From Athletes to Zebras—Young Children Want to Read About Them." *Elementary English* 52:73–78.

Laney, J., and P. Mosely. 1990. "Who Packed the Suitcase?: Playing the Role of an Archeologist/ Anthropologist." *Social Studies and the Young Learner,* 17–19.

Langer, J. A. 1992. "Reading, Writing and Genre Development." In *Reading/Writing Connection: Learning from Research,* ed. J. Irwin and M. Doyle, 32–54. Newark, DE: International Reading Association.

Lemke, J. 1992. "Intertextuality and Educational Research." *Linguistics and Education* 4: 257–68.

Lenters, K. 2004/2005. "No Half-Measures: Reading Instruction for Young Second-Language Learners." *Reading Teacher* 58(4): 328–36.

Lesaux, N. and L. Siegel. 2003. "The Development of Reading in Children Who Speak English as a Second Language." *Developmental Pyschology* 39(6): 1005–101.

McCullough, D. 2001. *John Adams.* New York: Simon and Schuster.

McGee, L. 1982. "Awareness of Text Structure: Effects on Children's Recall of Expository Text." *Reading Research Quarterly.* 17:581–90.

McKeough, A. 1984. "Developmental Stages in Children's Narrative Composition." ERIC Document Reproduction Service No. ED 249 461.

Meet the Author series. Katonah, NY: Richard C. Owens.

Meier, D. 2004. "The Young Child's Memory for Words: Developing First and Second Language and Literacy." New York: Teachers College Press.

Meltzer, M. 1988. *Starting from Home: A Writer's Beginnings.* New York: Viking Penguin.

Meyer, B. 1975. *The Organization of Prose and Its Effects on Memory.* Amsterdam: North-Holland.

Meyer, B., D. Brandt, and G. Bluth. 1980. "Use of Top-Level Structure in Text: Key for Reading Comprehension of Ninth-Grade Students." *Reading Research Quarterly* 16(1): 72–103.

Monson, D., and S. Sebesta. 1991. "Reading Preferences." In *Handbook of Research on Teaching the English Language Arts,* ed. J. Flood, J. Jensen, D. Lapp, and J. Squire, 664–73. New York: Macmillan.

Pappas, C. 1993. "Is Narrative 'Primary'? Some Insights from Kindergartners' Pretend Readings of Stories and Information Books." *Journal of Reading Behavior* 25(1): 97–129.

Paratore, J. 2000. "Grouping for Instruction in Reading: What We've Learned About What's Working and What's Not." *The California Reader* 33(4): 2–10.

Portalupi, J., and R. Fletcher. 2001. *Nonfiction Craft Lessons: Teaching Information Writing K–8*. Portland, ME: Stenhouse.

Raphael, Englert, and Kirschner. 1989. "Students' Metacognitive Knowledge about Writing." *Research in the Teaching of English* 23: 343–79.

Robb, L. 2004. *Nonfiction Writing: From the Inside Out*. New York: Scholastic.

Roop, P. 1992. "Nonfiction Books in the Primary Classroom: Soaring with the Swans." In *Using Nonfiction Trade Books in the Elementary Classroom: From Ants to Zeppelins*, ed. E. B. Freeman and D. G. Person, 106–12. Urbana, IL: National Council for Teachers of English.

Rosenblatt, L. 1978. *The Reader, the Text, the Poem: The Transactional Theory of the Literary Work*. Carbondale: Southern Illinois University Press.

———. 1988. "Writing and Reading: The Transactional Theory." *Reader* 20: 7–31.

———. 1991a. "Literary Theory." In *Handbook on Teaching the English Language Arts Process*, ed. J. Flood, J. Jensen, D. Lapp, and J. Squire, 57–62. New York: Macmillan.

———. 1991b. "The Reading Transaction: What For?" In *Literacy in Process*, ed. B. Power and R. Hubbard, 114–27. Portsmouth, NH: Heinemann.

Russell, D. L. 1991. *Literature for Children: A Short Introduction*. New York: Longman.

Short, K. 1992. "Researching Intertextuality Within Collaborative Classroom Learning Environments." *Linguistics and Education* 4: 257–68.

Simpson, A. 1996. "Fictions and Facts: An Investigation of Reading Practices of Girls and Boys." *English Education* 2(4): 268–79.

Smith, M. W., and J. D. Wilhelm. 2002. *Reading Don't Fix No Chevys: Literacy in the Lives of Young Men*. Portsmouth, NH: Heinemann.

Snow, C., M. S. Burns, and P. Griffin. 1998. *Preventing Reading Difficulties in Young Children*. Washington, DC: National Academy Press.

Something About the Author, autobiography series. Detroit, MI: Gale Research.

Spink, J. K. 1996. "The Aesthetics of Informational Reading." *The New Advocate* 9(2): 135–49.

Stead, T. 2002. *Is That a Fact? Teaching Nonfiction Writing K–3*. Portland, ME: Stenhouse.

Stein, N. and C. Glenn. 1979. "An Analysis of Story Comprehension in Elementary School Children." In *New Directions in Discourse Processing*, ed. R. Freedle, 53-129. Norwood, NJ: Ablex.

Sutherland, Z. 1997. *Children and Books*. 9th ed. New York: Longman.

Taylor, B., and R. Beach, 1984. "The Effects of Text Structure Instruction on Middle-Grade Students' Comprehension and Production of Expository Text." *Reading Research Quarterly* 19: 147–61.

Weidensaul, S. 2004. "The Most Resonant Book I Have Read." In *Remarkable Reads: 34 Writers and Their Adventures in Reading*, ed. J. P. Zane, 51–58. New York: W. W. Norton.

Weizman, Z., and C. Snow. 2001. "Lexical Input Related to Children's Vocabulary Acquisition: Effects of Sophisticated Exposure and Support for Meaning." *Developmental Psychology* 37: 265–79.

Wong-Fillmore, L., and C. Snow. 2002. "What Teachers Need to Know About Language." In *What Teachers Need to Know About Language*, ed. C. Temple Adger, C. Snow and D. Christian, 7–53. Washington, DC: Center for Applied Linguistics.

Worthy, J., M. Moorman, and M. Turner. 1999. "What Johnny Likes to Read: The Importance of Opportunity, Choice, and Access." *Reading Research Quarterly* 34(1): 12–27.

Yolen, J. 1991. "The Route to Story." *The New Advocate* 4: 143–49.

Zane, J. P. 2004. "The Hippest Book I Have Read." In *Remarkable Reads: 34 Writers and Their Adventures in Reading,* ed. J. P. Zane, 105–110. New York: W. W. Norton.

Children's Literature Cited

Baylor, B. 1986. *I'm in Charge of Celebrations*. New York: Simon and Schuster.

Cole, J. 1971. *Cock Roaches*. New York: William Morrow.

———. 1976. *A Chick Hatches*. New York: William Morrow.

———. 1981. *A Snake's Body*. New York: William Morrow.

———. 1986. *Hungry, Hungry Sharks*. New York: Random House.

Esbensen, B. 1986. *Words with Wrinkled Knees: Animal Poems*. New York: Crowell.

Gibbons, G. 1987. *The Pottery Place*. New York: Harcourt Brace.

———. 1991a. *From Seed to Plant*. New York: Holiday House.

———. 1991b. *Whales*. New York: Holiday House.

London, J. 1996. *Froggy Goes to School*. New York, NY: Penguin.

Maestro, B. 1990. *A Sea Full of Sharks*. New York: Scholastic.

Morris, A. 1990. *Loving*. New York: Harper Collins.

———. 1992. *Tools*. New York: Harper Collins.

———. 1995. *Weddings*. New York: Harper Collins.

———. 1996. *Karate Boy*. New York: Dutton Children's Books.

———. 2003. *That's our Teacher!* Minneapolis: Lerner Books.

———. 2003. *That's our Principal!* Minneapolis: Lerner Books.

———. 2003. *That's our Librarian!* Minneapolis: Lerner Books.

———. 2003. *That's our Gym Teacher!* Minneapolis: Lerner Books.

———. 2003. *That's our Custodian!* Minneapolis: Lerner Books.

———. 2003. *That's our Nurse!* Minneapolis: Lerner Books.

Simon, S. 1982. *The Smallest Dinosaurs*. New York: Crown.

———. 1986. *The Largest Dinosaurs*. New York: Macmillan.

———. 1990. *New Questions and Answers About Dinosaurs*. New York: Morrow.

Stanley, D. 1997. *Leonardo Da Vinci*. New York: Morrow.

Symes, R. F. 1988. *Rocks and Minerals*. New York: Dorling Kindersley.

Tarcov, E. 1974. *The Frog Prince*. New York: Scholastic.

Wick, W. 1997. *A Drop of Water*. New York: Scholastic.

Appendix A:
Curriculum Maps

ESSENTIAL QUESTIONS
Who is Gail Gibbons?
What do good readers do to actively and strategically process nonfiction text?
What can Gail Gibbons teach us about writing nonfiction?

Interplay of Multiple Responses	Books Used	Other Resources	Content/Skills, Frameworks	Assessment
Biographical Why would Gail Gibbons write two books on apples?	*The Seasons of Arnold's Apple Tree* *Apples*	Internet information	Make predictions and inferences. Ask questions. MA/ELA: 2.2, 8.15, 13.3 IRA/NCTE: 3, 11	Brainstorm and document ideas.
Personal Is our school apple tree like the ones in Gail Gibbons' books?	*The Seasons of Arnold's Apple Trees* *Apples*	Sample friendly letter format Samples of journal entries	Write for a specific purpose. Keep a journal. Determine sequence, visualize, compare and contrast. MA/ELA: 2.2, 8.16, 10.2, 15.2, 19.13 IRA/NCTE: 4, 6, 7 MA/STE: 3, 4, 7, 8	Compose letter to principal asking for tree help. Journal entries (written and illustrated) on apple tree observations through-out the year
Biographical What does Gail Gibbons write about?	Large collection of Gibbons books	Sample bar graph	Sort, categorize, and graph information. Pose questions and discuss. MA/ELA: 2.2, 8.15, 13.7 IRA/NCTE: 1, 6, 7, 11	Book category web Bar graph
Biographical Who is Gail Gibbons?		Internet sites	Locate data on the Internet. Create informational web. Summarize information. MA/ELA: 8.15, 8.18, 19.11 IRA/NCTE: 1, 4, 7, 12	Generate a biographical web. Contribute to whole-class discussion. Create biographical acrostic poem. Play biography game: *Jeopardy* in PowerPoint.
Personal What experiences have you had with frogs? What do you know about frogs?	*Frogs*	*The Frog Prince* (Tor-cov 1974) *Froggy Goes to School* (London 1996) Discovery Channel	Make personal connections to text. Build personal schemata. Distinguish fact from opinion. MA/ELA: 2.2, 13.7 IRA/NCTE: 11, 12 MA/STE: 1, 3, 4, 6, 7, 8	Contribute ideas to class KWL chart on frogs.
Text Based What is "metacognition?	*Frogs* *The Pumpkin Book* *Thanksgiving Is* *Pigs* *Chicks and Chickens* *Christmas Is* *Soaring With the Wind: Bald Eagles* *Rabbits, Rabbits, and More Rabbits* *Penguins*	*Little Me on my shoulder* Variety of read-aloud books	Use self-questioning. Monitor for understanding. MA/ELA: 8.15 IRA/NCTE: 3	Observe active thinking to make meaning as students ask themselves questions such as: Does it make sense to me? Am I wondering about what I am hearing?

Interplay of Multiple Responses	Books Used	Other Resources	Content/Skills, Frameworks	Assessment
Text Based *What do good readers do before, during, and after reading?*	Variety of Gail Gibbons books	Explicit modeling during interactive read-alouds; Gradual release model chart; Anchor charts; Anticipation guide on *Pumpkins*	Determine the purpose for the text. Make personal connections. Activate prior knowledge. Develop questions. Use text features to find information. Make predictions and inferences. Visualize. Reflect. Summarize. Use fix-up strategies. Retell main ideas and important facts. MA/ELA: 8.18, 8.21, 8.22, 13.3, 13.4, 13.5, 13.7, 13.15 IRA/NCTE: 3, 4, 6, 11, 12	Observe use of modeled reading strategies. Construct graphic organizers on various animal/book topics. Participate in turn-and-talk pair-share activity. Complete Anticipation guide on *Pumpkins*. Construct animal classification chart on frog, bald eagle, polar bear, and monarch butterfly.
Text Based *What text structures and text features does Gail Gibbons use to present and organize information in her books?*	*Frogs*; *The Pumpkin Book*; *The Seasons of Arnold's Apple Tree*; *Monarch Butterfly*; *Soaring With the Wind: Bald Eagles*; *Pandas*; *Chicks and Chickens*	Graphic organizers of text structure types; List of text features observed during book readings	Analyze nonfiction text structures: *sequence, description, cause and effect, compare and contrast, and problem and solution.* Analyze nonfiction text features: *bold/italic type, labels, diagrams, charts, graphs, captions, maps, headings, print color, inserts, cross sections, bullets.* MA/ELA: 2.2, 8.16, 8.21, 8.22, 13.7, 13.15 IRA/NCTE: 1, 3, 6, 11	Decorate a pumpkin and write a clear *description. Sequence* illustrations of apple tree development throughout a year. Label diagrams and *sequence* frog and butterfly stages of development. Complete a *cause-and-effect* graphic organizer on bald eagles. Develop gist statements about the five types of text structures and various text features observed. Participate in turn-and-talk pair-share activity.
Culminating Project *How can we emulate Gail Gibbons as nonfiction authors and illustrators?*	*Ranger Rick*; *National Geographic for Kids*; *Animals of the World*; Variety of animal books; Encyclopedias	Computer software: Kidspiration; Scholastic Keys; PowerPoint; Internet sites on specific animals; Writing template	Research an animal of interest. Generate questions to research. Collect, organize, and present information. Present in both efferent and aesthetic ways. MA/ELA: 2.2, 3.4, 8.15, 8.18, 8.21, 8.22, 13.5, 13.9, 19.11, 23.2, 24.1, 24.2 IRA/NCTE: 1, 3, 4, 6, 12 MA/STE (Gr. PreK-2): *1, 3, 4, 6, 7, 8	Complete animal web template for selected animal. Create two PowerPoint slides: written paragraph of information and an illustration. Present PowerPoint slides to audience with appropriate fluency and volume.
Culminating Project *How can we share some of the information we've learned with our school and families?*	*Monarch Butterfly*	*Betty Butterfly's Welcome Home Party*: play script; Butterfly song	Perform a play for an audience. MA/ELA: 2.2, 3.4, 10.2, 15.2 IRA/NCTE: 4, 6, 12	Create costumes and scenery to fit the play events. Participate in presenting the play; speak with appropriate fluency and volume.

*MA/STE: Application of MA Science and Technology/Engineering Standards varies based on content relevant to students' research questions.

ESSENTIAL QUESTIONS
Who is Ann Morris?
Why does Ann Morris write books about places all over the world?
How can an author study promote literacy development in English language learners?
What can Ann Morris teach us about writing nonfiction?

Interplay of Multiple Responses	Books Used	Other Resources	Content/Skills, Frameworks	Assessment
Personal How do people travel in the United States and in other countries?	On the Go	Venn diagram Sticky notes for note taking	Contribute knowledge to class discussion. Relate themes in nonfiction to personal experience. Make predictions about the content of the text using illustrations. Locate facts that answer the reader's questions. MA/ELA: 2.1 8.4, 8.15, 11.1 IRA/NCTE: 3, 11, 12	In small groups, take notes about On the Go. Place notes on a Venn diagram to show similarities and differences. Share notes and Venn diagram with others.
Text Based How do I find information in nonfiction texts?	On the Go	World map	Identify and use textual and graphic features. On a world map, locate the country you or your ancestors came from. MA/ELA: 13.1, 13.2 IRA/NCTE: 3	Use the index to find out additional information about a picture in the text. Locate your native country on a world map.
Personal When have you been part of a team?	Play Teamwork	Writing prompt	Make predictions about the content of the text using illustrations. Relate themes in nonfiction to personal experience. MA/ELA: 8.4, 11.1 IRA/NCTE: 12	Share personal experiences related to the text with others orally. Write about at least one experience.
Text Based How do you write a research question and gather information?	Houses and Homes Bread, Bread, Bread Shoes, Shoes, Shoes	Resources to model note taking	Write a research question. Record notes from information in a text. MA/ELA: 19.8 IRA/NCTE: 7	Participate as class writes research questions for each book. Read a book and take notes to answer the research question.
Text Based How do you clearly communicate to others what you have learned?	Notes from Houses and Homes Bread, Bread, Bread Shoes, Shoes, Shoes		Write a brief summary of information gathered. Reform research question into the topic sentence. MA/ELA: 19.11 IRA/NCTE: 7	Using your notes, write some complete sentences about the information. Form a paragraph with a topic sentence, supporting details, and a concluding sentence.

Interplay of Multiple Responses	Books Used	Other Resources	Content/Skills, Frameworks	Assessment
Personal What memorable experiences have you had with a family member?	*Grandma Francisca Remembers* *Grandma Lai Goon Remembers*	Children's family photographs Assorted magazine pictures	Relate themes in nonfiction to personal experience. Write a short account of a personal experience that follows a logical order. MA/ELA: 11.1, 19.7 IRA/NCTE: 4, 7	Orally share a personal experience about family life or your experience with a family member. Write a short story describing an event or person in a photograph or other picture.
Personal What special thing did you do with or learn from someone on your family tree?	*Grandma Lois Remembers*	Family tree worksheet	Make predictions about the content of the text using prior knowledge and text features. Relate themes in nonfiction to personal experience. MA/ELA: 8.4, 11.1 IRA/NCTE: 4, 7	With help at home, write the names of family members on your family tree. Write about something special you did with or learned from a person on your family tree.
Text Based What are the steps for making a recipe or doing something?	*What Was It Like, Grandma? books- Grandma . . . Remembers*	How-to graphic organizer	Arrange events in order when writing. Arrange ideas in a way that makes sense. MA/ELA: 23.1, 23.2 IRA/NCTE: 4	Brainstorm three ideas for your how-to paper. Select one idea and list the steps for doing it. Create a graphic organizer as an aid. Write an explanation of the task.
Biographical Who is Ann Morris?	Reference to many of Ann Morris' books	Biographical information about Ann Morris	Pose questions. Synthesize information. MA/ELA: 9.1, 9.3 IRA/NCTE: 7, 11	Contribute ideas and questions to discussion about the author.
Culminating Project How can Ann Morris' writing styles help me write a country book?	Ann Morris' books	Ann Morris class map Interviews Photographs Internet resources	Identify and apply steps in conducting and reporting research questions. Locate facts that answer the reader's questions. Write summaries of information gathered through research. Identify and describe traditions, customs, well-known sites, events, and landmarks in my country. Use written and visual language to accomplish your own purposes. MA/ELA: 8.15, 24.1, 24.2, 19.11, 21.2, 23.2 MA/HSS:* 2.1, 2.7, 2.8, 2.9 IRA/NCTE: 11, 12	On a world map, locate the country you will write about in your book. Contribute to the list of items that could be included in the country book. Read and take notes on information to answer your questions. Read and record information about traditions, customs, well-known sites, events, and landmarks in my country. Include organizational features of the book (e.g., table of contents, index). Bind the completed book and share it with others.

*MA/HSS: Application of MA History and Social Science Standards varies based on the country the student researches.

ESSENTIAL QUESTIONS

Who is Jim Arnosky?
Have you ever caught a frog?
How do features of nonfiction text help us communicate clearly?
What can Jim Arnosky teach us about writing nonfiction?

Interplay of Multiple Responses	Books Used	Other Resources	Content/Skills, Frameworks	Assessment
Biographical Who packed the suitcase?	Selected books by Jim Arnosky	Suitcase packed with items representing Arnosky's life and work; Inference template	Ask questions, make predictions, confirm or reject MA/ELA: 8.4, 13.3 IRA/NCTE: 3, 11 MA/STE (Gr. 3–5):* Inquiry Skills	Document items found in the suitcase and then use this evidence to make inferences about who packed the suitcase.
Text Based What would you expect to see in nonfiction books?	Selection of nonfiction trade books, such as *Rocks and Minerals* (Symes 1988), *A Drop of Water* (Wick 1997), *Leonardo Da Vinci* (Stanley 1997)	Reading train strategy	Identify and use common textual features, graphic features, and organizational structures. MA/ELA: 8.21, 13.1, 13.2, 13.6, 13.7, 13.8, 13.15 IRA/NCTE: 3, 6	Contribute to class list of features of nonfiction books.
Text Based What text features does Jim Arnosky use in his books?	Large number of books by Arnosky representing different series and themes	Few nonfiction books by other children's authors	Identify and use common textual features, graphic features, and organizational structures. MA/ELA: 8.21, 13.1, 13.2, 13.6, 13.7, 13.8, 13.15 IRA/NCTE: 3, 6	Contribute to class list of features that are most common in Arnosky's books.
Personal What experiences have you, or someone you know, had with a frog? What do you know about frogs?	*All About Frogs*	Anticipation guide	Relate books to personal experience. Tap prior knowledge of subject matter to make predictions. MA/ELA: 11.1, 13.3, 23.5 IRA/NCTE: 4, 11	Write about a personal (or secondhand) experience with a frog. Prereading: Using prior knowledge, complete the anticipation guide about frogs. Post-reading: Use facts in the text to review and correct anticipation guide.
Text Based What is a heading? How are headings useful?	*All About Frogs* Other series books: *All About Alligators* *All About Deer* *All About Owls* *All About Rattlesnakes* *All About Turtles*	Paragraphs or pages of text from other nonfiction books	Summarize main ideas and supporting details. Identify and use common textual features *(including headings).* Restate main ideas and important facts. MA/ELA: 8.18, 13.1, 13.5 IRA/NCTE: 3, 11	With a partner, write a meaningful heading for one or more pages of *All About Frogs.* Independently write meaningful headings for all pages of another book in the All About series.

Interplay of Multiple Responses	Books Used	Other Resources	Content/Skills, Frameworks	Assessment
Text Based What are topic sentences? Why are they important?	All About Frogs All About Sharks	"On My Hand!" worksheet	Identify and analyze main ideas, supporting ideas, and supporting details. Identify and use common textual features (including topic sentences). MA/ELA: 8.22, 13.6 IRA/NCTE: 3	Given details on a subject, write a topic sentence that captures the main idea.
Text Based What is paraphrasing?	All About Frogs Other All About series books	Green construction paper for pamphlets	Paraphrase by restating main ideas and facts. MA/ELA: 13.5 IRA/NCTE: 4, 7 MA/STE (Gr. 3–5):* 3, 6, 7	Create a "Five Frog Facts" pamphlet. Be sure to paraphrase information and cite author.
Culminating Project: Report Writing What is important to know and tell others about species that are endangered in our world today?	Arnosky's Ark Other nonfiction books on identified endangered species	Categorized list of endangered species not included in Arnosky's Ark Many books and resource materials gathered from the classroom, library, and Internet Note-taking worksheet	Generate basic research questions and gather information from several sources. Distinguish fact from opinion. Write brief summaries of information gathered through research. Cite sources. Edit and revise. MA/ELA: 2.2, 13.5, 13.9, 13.11, 13.12, 19.11, 21.2, 24.1, 24.2, 24.3 IRA/NCTE: 6, 7, 11, 12 MA/STE (Gr. 3–5): * 1, 3, 5, 6, 7, 8, Inquiry Skills	Research an endangered species. Write research notes about important facts and key reasons for its endangerment. Record data carefully. Paraphrase information. Cite sources. Use research notes to write a paragraph about the endangered species. Edit and revise the report. Draw an illustration of the endangered species. Contribute your report to the class Ark book. Contribute ideas to writing the class dedication and introduction to the Ark book.
Video Presentation What is the most interesting or important fact about my endangered species?	Class book titled Animal Ark	Video equipment	Give oral presentations using eye contact, proper place, adequate volume, and clear pronunciation. MA/ELA: 3.4 IRA/NCTE: 12	Orally present information about one endangered species for the class video of the Ark book.
Biographical What kind of person and writer is Jim Arnosky?	Large number of books by Arnosky (previously used) representing different series and themes	Hunch tree and leafy notes	Make predictions; confirm or reject. MA/ELA: 13.3, 13.4 IRA/NCTE: 3, 11	Contribute hunches about Jim Arnosky to the class hunch tree. Determine which hunches are accurate and which are incorrect.
Culminating Project: Biographical Who is Jim Arnosky? What do we know about him as a person and a writer?	Author information found in many books by Jim Arnosky	Jim Arnosky's Outdoor Journal website at www.jimarnosky.com Semantic map for class note taking	Organize information about a topic into a coherent paragraph. MA/ELA: 8.17, 9.3, 13.1, 13.2, 13.6, 13.7, 13.8, 13.11, 13.15, 19.11, 23.7, 23.8 IRA/NCTE: 3, 11, 12	Work with a team to research and write a biography of Jim Arnosky. Include facts about his life, his books, and his hobbies. Create a cover and bind the book. Share with your class.

*MA/STE: Application of MA Science and Technology/Engineering Standards varies based on content relevant to students' research questions.

ESSENTIAL QUESTIONS
Who is Jean Fritz?
Why is Jean Fritz so interested in the events and people involved in American history?
What can Jean Fritz teach us about writing nonfiction?

Interplay of Multiple Responses	Books Used	Other Resources	Content/Skills, Frameworks	Assessment
Biographical Who is Jean Fritz?	*Homesick* (Fritz 1982)	Bulletin board with photo of Jean Fritz and speech bubbles	Distinguish fact from opinion. Relate themes to personal experience. MA/ELA: 11.1, 13.11 IRA/NCTE: 1, 11	Discuss key episode in Fritz's life; evoke personal responses.
Personal Have you ever daydreamed?	*Can't You Make Them Behave, King George?*		Relate themes in nonfiction to personal experience. MA/ELA: 11.1 IRA/NCTE: 1, 11	Share your thoughts with others.
Text Based What are the characteristics of a good biography?	*Can't You Make Them Behave, King George?*		Distinguish among forms of literature such as poetry, prose, fiction, nonfiction, and drama and apply this knowledge as a strategy for reading and writing. Apply knowledge of genre to create, critique, and discuss print texts. MA/ELA: 10.2 IRA/NCTE: 1, 6	Contribute to the class list of characteristics of a good biography. Assess whether this book has the characteristics of a good biography.
Text Based Can you distinguish between fact and opinion?	*George Washington's Mother*	"Facts and Personal Traits" two-column graphic organizer	Distinguish fact from opinion or fiction. Be reflective and critical about the texts you read. MA/ELA: 8.17, 13.11 IRA/NCTE: 11 MA/HSS*: 3.7 (M. Washington)	Complete the two-column graphic organizer by identifying facts and character traits of Martha Washington.
Text Based What makes a great biography?	*George Washington's Mother And Then What Happened, Paul Revere?*	Sentence strips of selected events from the Paul Revere biography	Identify common organizational structures (*chronological order*). Arrange events in order when writing or dictating. Recognize that a biography is a careful selection of facts that bring a character to life, including personal facts, traits, important influences, obstacles, and accomplishments. MA/ELA: 13.8, 23.1, 13.11 IRA/NCTE: 3, 6 MA/HSS*: 3.5 (Paul Revere)	Assess whether a text follows a chronological order. Identify time-order words (e.g., *first, then, next, finally*). Place events from a biography in chronological order. Write one fact of each type from your own life and place it into the appropriate category.

Interplay of Multiple Responses	Books Used	Other Resources	Content/Skills, Frameworks	Assessment
Text Based What stylistic devices does Jean Fritz use to engage readers?	*And Then What Happened, Paul Revere?* *Why Don't You Get a Horse, Sam Adams?* *Will You Sign Here, John Hancock?*		Identify and use knowledge of common textual features. Use knowledge of language structure, language conventions, figurative language, and genre to create, critique, and discuss print texts. Explain important political, economic, and military developments leading to and during the American Revolution. MA/ELA: 9.1, 13.1 IRA/NCTE: 6 MA/HSS: * 3.5 (Paul Revere, Sam Adams, John Hancock)	Identify ways that Jean Fritz uses repetition, humor, and different voices to capture readers' attention. Identify any other stylistic devices she uses to inform and entertain her readers.
Culminating Project: Colonial Tea Party If you lived in colonial times, who would you be? What would you look like? What would you do? How would you talk?	Reference all books used during the author study		Contribute knowledge to class discussion to develop ideas for a class project. Give oral presentations about interests using eye contact, proper place, adequate volume, and clear pronunciation. Organize ideas related to a personal experience in a way that makes sense. Use spoken and visual language to accomplish your own purpose. Adjust your spoken language to communicate effectively with a variety of audiences and for different purposes. After reading a biography, summarize the person's life and achievements. MA/ELA: 2.1, 11.1, 23.5 IRA/NCTE: 4, 12 MA/HSS: 3.7	Portray a patriot or a patriot's family member whom we have studied. Prepare to portray using appropriate attire, behavior and manners, language, and prepared topics of conversation.

*MA/HSS: Application of MA History and Social Science Standards varies based on the historical person studied.

ESSENTIAL QUESTIONS
Who is Sandra Markle?
Have you ever seen a snake? Shark? Alligator?
What can Sandra Markle teach us about writing nonfiction?

Interplay of Multiple Responses	Books Used	Other Resources	Content/Skills, Frameworks	Assessment
Biographical Who is Sandra Markle?	*Words with Wrinkled Knees: Animal Poems* (Esbensen 1986) *I'm in Charge of Celebrations* (Baylor 1986)	Sandra Markle posters Poetry riddles to predict topics of Markle's books	Make inferences about Markle. Research inferences on Internet. MA/ELA: 2.2, 13.7 IRA/NCTE: 1, 7, 11	Contribute research findings to class KWL chart (modified).
Personal Have you ever seen a snake? What do you think you know about snakes?	*Outside and Inside Snakes*	Teacher's personal response Anticipation guide	Offer personal connections to topic. Tap prior knowledge. MA/ELA: 8.9, 15.2, 19.13 IRA/NCTE: 1, 4	Write and share a personal response. Complete first part of anticipation guide.
Text Based What did you learn about snakes? Can you become an expert and write an anticipation guide for peers to complete?	*Outside and Inside Snakes* Choose an Outside and Inside book such as *Alligators and Crocodiles*, *Sharks*, or *Dinosaurs*	Checklist for designing an anticipation guide	Comprehend and recall main ideas and details. Write effective items. MA/ELA: 8.15, 8.16, 8.18, 8.22, 13.17, 19.11, 24.2 IRA/NCTE: 1, 3, 11 MA/STE (Gr. 3–5):* 4, 5, 6, 8	Complete second part of anticipation guide. Write anticipation guide for a book of your choice and place on the Markle table for peers to complete.
Text-Based How does Sandra Markle organize her information?	*Outside and Inside Snakes* *Growing Up Wild: Bears* *After the Spill: The Exxon Valdez Disaster, Then and Now*		Differentiate fiction and nonfiction text structures. Analyze nonfiction text structures (compare and contrast, sequence, and description) at top level and paragraph level. Identify signal words for each text structure. MA/ELA: 8.21, 8.22, 10.2, 13.15, 13.17 IRA/NCTE: 3, 6	Complete a Venn diagram for one compare-and-contrast section of a selected book; complete graphic organizers for other text structures.

Interplay of Multiple Responses	Books Used	Other Resources	Content/Skills, Frameworks	Assessment
Personal and Text Based How can I persuade peers to read other Sandra Markle books?	After the Spill: The Exxon Valdez Disaster, Then and Now Choice of Markle books	Book talk guidelines	Use persuasion. Involve audience. Summarize information. Present information clearly. MA/ELA: 3.3, 3.4, 3.12, 3.13 IRA/NCTE: 4, 11, 12 MA/STE (Gr. 3–5): * 4, 5, 6, 8	Present a book talk to peers; videotape the presentation.
Biographical Did you know that Sandra Markle . . . ? More about the person and the writer		Biographical information from a variety of sources	Pose questions. Synthesize information. MA/ELA: 2.2 IRA/NCTE: 4, 7	Generate written questions to use during an "interview" with Sandra Markle.
Culminating Project How can we tell Sandra Markle that we like her books?		Biopoem frame	Distill important information. MA/ELA: 2.2 IRA/NCTE: 7, 11, 12	Write Sandra Markle biopoem; post and send to author.

*MA/STE: Application of MA Science and Technology/Engineering Standards varies based on specific content of the selected text.

Appendix B:
Selected Curriculum Standards

Massachusetts Department of Education:
English Language Arts Curriculum Frameworks (2001)

General Standard 2: Questioning, Listening, and Contributing

MA/ELA: 2.1   Contribute knowledge to class discussion in order to develop ideas for a class project.

MA/ELA: 2.2   Contribute knowledge to class discussion in order to develop ideas for a class project and generate interesting questions to be used as part of the project.

General Standard 3: Oral Presentation

MA/ELA: 3.4   Give oral presentations about experiences or interests using eye contact, proper place, adequate volume, and clear pronunciation.

MA/ELA: 3.12   Give oral presentations to different audiences for various purposes, showing appropriate changes in delivery and using language for dramatic effect.

MA/ELA: 3.13   Create a scoring guide based on categories supplied by the teacher to prepare and assess their presentations.

General Standard 8: Understanding a Text

MA/ELA: 8.4   Make predictions about the content of the text using prior knowledge and text features (*title, captions, illustrations*).

MA/ELA: 8.15   Locate facts that answer the reader's questions.

MA/ELA: 8.16   Distinguish cause from effect.

MA/ELA: 8.17   Distinguish fact from opinion or fiction.

MA/ELA: 8.18   Summarize main ideas and supporting details.

MA/ELA: 8.21   Recognize organizational structures (*chronological order, logical order, cause and effect, classification schemes*).

MA/ELA: 8.22   Identify and analyze main ideas, supporting ideas, and supporting details.

General Standard 9: Making Connections

MA/ELA: 9.1   Identify similarities in plot, setting, and character among the works of an author or illustrator.

MA/ELA: 9.3   Identify similarities and differences between the characters or events in a literary work and the actual experiences in an author's life.

General Standard 10: Genre

MA/ELA: 10.2   Distinguish among forms of literature such as poetry, prose, fiction, nonfiction, and drama and apply this knowledge as a strategy for reading and writing.

General Standard 11: Theme

MA/ELA: 11.1   Relate themes in works of fiction and nonfiction to personal experience.

General Standard 13: Nonfiction

MA/ELA: 13.1   Identify and use knowledge of common textual features (*title, headings, captions, key words, table of contents*).

MA/ELA: 13.2   Identify and use knowledge of common graphic features (*illustrations, type size*).

MA/ELA: 13.3   Make predictions about the content of a text using prior knowledge and text and graphic features.

MA/ELA: 13.4   Explain whether predictions about the content of a text were confirmed or disconfirmed and why.

MA/ELA: 13.5   Restate main ideas and important facts from a text heard or read.

MA/ELA: 13.6   Identify and use knowledge of common textual features (*paragraphs, topic sentences, concluding sentences, glossary*).

MA/ELA: 13.7   Identify and use knowledge of common graphic features (*charts, maps, diagrams, illustrations*).

MA/ELA: 13.8   Identify and use knowledge of common organizational structures (*chronological order*).

MA/ELA: 13.9   Locate facts that answer the reader's questions.

MA/ELA: 13.10 Distinguish cause from effect.

MA/ELA: 13.11 Distinguish fact from opinion or fiction.

MA/ELA: 13.12 Summarize main ideas and supporting details.

MA/ELA: 13.15 Identify and use knowledge of common organizational structures (*chronological order, logical order, cause and effect, classification schemes*).

General Standard 15: Style and Language

MA/ELA: 15.2 Identify words appealing to the senses or involving direct comparisons in literature and spoken language.

General Standard 19: Writing

MA/ELA: 19.7 Write or dictate letters, directions, or short accounts of personal experiences that follow a logical order.

MA/ELA: 19.8 Write or dictate research questions.

MA/ELA: 19.11 Write brief summaries of information gathered through research.

MA/ELA: 19.13 Write an account based on personal experience that has a clear focus and sufficient supporting detail.

General Standard 21: Revising

MA/ELA: 21.2 Revise writing to improve level of detail after determining what could be added or deleted.

General Standard 23: Organizing Ideas in Writing

MA/ELA: 23.1 Arrange events in order when writing or dictating.

MA/ELA: 23.2 Arrange ideas in a way that makes sense.

MA/ELA: 23.4 Organize ideas for a brief response to a reading.

MA/ELA: 23.5 Organize ideas for an account of personal experience in a way that makes sense.

General Standard 24: Research

MA/ELA: 24.1 Generate questions and gather information from several sources in a classroom, school, or public library.

MA/ELA: 24.2 Identify and apply steps in conducting and reporting research questions.

MA/ELA: 24.3 Apply steps for obtaining information from a variety of sources, organizing information, documenting sources, and presenting research in individual and group projects.

International Reading Association/National Council of Teachers of English: Standards for the English Language Arts (1996)

IRA/NCTE: 1	Students read a wide range of print and non-print texts to build an understanding of texts, of themselves, to acquire new information, and for personal fulfillment.
IRA/NCTE: 3	Students apply a wide range of strategies to comprehend, interpret, evaluate, and appreciate texts. They draw on their prior experience, their interactions with other readers and writers, their knowledge of word meaning and of other texts, their word identification strategies, and their understanding of textual features.
IRA/NCTE: 4	Students adjust their use of spoken, written, and visual language . . . to communicate effectively with a variety of audiences and for different purposes.
IRA/NCTE: 6	Students apply knowledge of language structure, language conventions . . . media techniques, figurative language, and genre to create, critique, and discuss print and non-print texts.
IRA/NCTE: 7	Students conduct research on issues and interests by generating ideas and questions, and by posing problems. They gather, evaluate, and synthesize data from a variety of sources . . . to communicate their discoveries in ways that suit their purpose and audience.
IRA/NCTE: 11	Students participate as knowledgeable, reflective, creative, and critical members of a variety of literacy communities.
IRA/NCTE: 12	Students use spoken, written, and visual language to accomplish their own purposes.

Massachusetts Department of Education: Science and Technology/Engineering Curriculum Frameworks (2001)

Life Science (Biology)—Grades PreK–2

MA/STE: 1	Recognize that animals (including humans) and plants are living things that grow, reproduce, and need food, air, and water.
MA/STE: 3	Recognize that plants and animals have life cycles, and that life cycles vary for different living things.
MA/STE: 4	Describe ways in which many plants and animals closely resemble their parents in observed appearance.
MA/STE: 6	Recognize that people and other animals interact with the environment through their senses of sight, hearing, touch, smell, and taste.
MA/STE: 7	Recognize changes in appearance that animals and plants go through as the seasons change.
MA/STE: 8	Identify ways in which an organism's habitat provides for its basic needs (plants require air, water, nutrients, and light; animals require food, water, air, and shelter).

Life Science (Biology)—Grades 3–5

MA/STE: 1   Classify plants and animals according to the physical characteristics that they share.

MA/STE: 3   Recognize that plants and animals go through predictable life cycles that include birth, growth, development, reproduction, and death.

MA/STE: 4   Describe the major stages that characterize the life cycle of the frog and butterfly as they go through metamorphosis.

MA/STE: 5   Differentiate between observed characteristics of plants and animals that are fully inherited and characteristics that are affected by the climate or environment.

MA/STE: 6   Give examples of how inherited characteristics may change over time as adaptations to changes in the environment that enable organisms to survive.

MA/STE: 7   Give examples of how changes in the environment have caused some plants and animals to die or move to new locations.

MA/STE: 8   Describe how organisms meet some of their needs in an environment by using behaviors (patterns of activities) in response to information (stimuli) received from the environment. Recognize that some animal behaviors are instinctive and others are learned.

Inquiry Skills—Grades 3–5

Ask questions and make predictions that can be tested.

Record data and communicate findings to others using graphs, charts, maps, models, and oral and written reports.

Massachusetts Department of Education: History and Social Science Curriculum Frameworks (2003)

Grade 2

MA/HSS: 2.1   On a map of the world, locate all the continents: North America, South America, Europe, Asia, Africa, Australia, and Antarctica. [Geography]

MA/HSS: 2.7   On a map of the world, locate the continent, regions, or and then the countries from which students, their parents, guardians, grandparents, or other relatives or ancestors came. With the help of family members and the school librarian, describe traditional food, customs, sports and games, and music of the place they came from. [Geography, Civics]

MA/HSS: 2.8   With the help of the school librarian, give examples of traditions or customs from other countries that can be found in America today. [Geography, Civics]

MA/HSS: 2.9   With the help of the school librarian, identify and describe well-known sites, events, or landmarks in at least three different countries from which students' families come and explain why they are important. [History, Geography, Civics]

Grade 3

MA/HSS: 3.5   Explain important political, economic, and military developments leading to and during the American Revolution—including: the Boston Tea Party; the beginning of the Revolution at Lexington and Concord; and Revolutionary leaders (e.g., John Adams, Samuel Adams, John Hancock, and Paul Revere). [History, Civics]

MA/HSS: 3.7   After reading a biography of a person from Massachusetts in one of the following categories, summarize the person's life and achievements (e.g., political). [History, Civics]

References

Massachusetts Department of Education. May 2001. *Massachusetts Science and Technology/Engineering Curriculum Framework.* Malden, MA: Commonwealth of Massachusetts Department of Education. Retrieved June 4, 2006, from http://www.doe.mass.edu/frameworks/scitech/2001/0501.pdf.

———. June 2001, May 2004 Supplement. *Massachusetts English Language Arts Curriculum Framework.* Malden, MA: Commonwealth of Massachusetts Department of Education. Retrieved June 4, 2006, from www.doe.mass.edu/frameworks/ela/0601.pdf.

———. August 2003. *Massachusetts History and Social Science Curriculum Framework.* Malden, MA: Commonwealth of Massachusetts Department of Education. Retrieved June 4, 2006, from www.doe.mass.edu/frameworks/hss/final.pdf.

National Council of Teachers of English (NCTE). 1996. *Standards for the English Language Arts.* Newark, DE: International Reading Association; Urbana, IL: NCTE. Retrieved March 26, 2006, from www.ncte.org/about/over/standards/110846.htm.

Appendix C:
Tips for Navigating the Internet

Deborah White

Internet Searching: Quick Tips for Hitting the Target

There are many popular *search engines* used to search the Internet. They include Google www.google.com, AltaVista www.altavista.com, Lycos www.lycos.com, Yahoo! www.yahoo.com, and many, many more. However, with the exponential growth of information, searching the World Wide Web can yield an unwieldy number of "hits," resulting in frustration and sometimes in getting hopelessly lost by following less-helpful links. Implementing the following search strategies will help you to narrow the search parameters and to be specific in your quest.

- Understand that a *basic search "string"* is made up of one or more words strung together to express the target of a search. Entering a couple of words or a short phrase will result in many hits or web pages found by the search. This may seem like a good thing, but in fact there will be many sites that are not at all related to what you really want to know, and it takes precious time to sort through these less-helpful sites. For example, entering the words <u>juvenile literature</u> will result in a list of hundreds of web pages that contain the words <u>juvenile</u> and/or <u>literature</u>, but there will be too many to be helpful and some will be completely off target.

- Use the *plus sign* to focus the search and find sites that include all of the target words. Adding additional parameters also serves to focus in on the search target. For example, the search string <u>juvenile +literature +nonfiction</u> locates sites with nonfiction literature for juveniles. In the same way, use the *minus sign* to focus the search by omitting sites with a specific word. The search string juvenile +literature +nonfiction –insect yields sites with nonfiction juvenile literature, but not about insects.

- Use *quotation marks* around a phrase to find sites that have the quoted words in that exact order, thereby greatly increasing the focus of the search. For example, the search string Sandra Markle yields hundreds of sites containing Sandra, many more with Markle, and a few with both—but you must sift through hundreds to find the few. You're more likely to find information on the author Sandra Markle by including quotes around the search string (i.e., "Sandra Markle"). There may be information on Sandra Markles who are not the author, but it will be a much shorter list. Additionally, *capitalization* is usually ignored by most search engines, so "Sandra Markle" and "SANDRA MARKLE" and "sandra markle" are all interpreted in lowercase and yield the same list of websites.

- *Combine functions* to further narrow searches and achieve an even greater focus. For example, the search string "sandra markle" +"outside and inside" lists websites with information about Sandra Markle's books in the Outside and Inside series. Similarly, "juvenile literature" +sharks hits sites with juvenile literature about sharks written by numerous authors. Searching for "sharks juvenile literature" on the Library of Congress website (www.loc.gov) yields 162 entries by Sandra Markle, Jim Arnosky, and numerous other authors. Searching for "sandra markle" +sharks narrows the search to just one author.

- Use the *advanced search functions* that the powerful search engines also offer. These often involve the use of *Boolean logic* commands that extend functions of the mathematical symbols (+ and –) found in basic search strings. For example, "juvenile literature" sharks OR bats locates websites with juvenile literature about either sharks or bats.

- Use the *specialized search capabilities* provided on most individual websites for libraries (e.g., Library of Congress www.loc.gov), publishing companies (e.g., www.barnesandnoble.com, www.simonsays.com, www.boydsmillspress.com, www.charlesbridge.com) and booksellers (e.g., www.amazon.com, www.biblio.com, www.strandbooks.com). Websites may provide prompts to suggest entries for search strings by category. For example, many booksellers invite users to browse by author, subject, or title by entering text into one of those three fields. Alternately, based on anticipated or actual search-history data, websites may create links to specific subsets of resources. For example, Boyds Mills Press provides links to categories such as picture books, nonfiction, poetry, and authors and illustrators (see www.boydsmillspress.com).

Implementing these basic Internet search strategies will help you become more adept at clarifying the target of each Internet search. Enjoy the journey and delight in the discovery!